BE THE CAUSE
HEALING HUMAN DISCONNECT

JUDY ROSENBERG, Ph.D.

Using the basic principles of attachment theory, combined with a 9-part technique for Mind Mapping, Judy Rosenberg, Ph.D. offers practical steps for healing old wounds. Whether you are single or in a committed relationship, if you are feeling disconnected, disempowered, or otherwise in pain, you will find something of value in *Be The Cause*.

-Stan Tatkin, PsyD, MFT

*"Wherever there is a human
being, there is an opportunity
for a kindness."*

-Lucius Anneaeus Seneca

ISBN: 0692108939
ISBN-13: 978-0692108932

Table Of Contents

DISCLAIMER

This book is not intended to be a substitute for professional medical advice, diagnosis, or treatment. Always seek the advice of your mental health provider with any questions you may have regarding a medical or psychological condition. Never disregard professional medical or psychological advice or delay in seeking it because of something you have read in this book. Dr. Judy Rosenberg and the Psychological Healing Center hereby disclaim any and all liability to any party for any direct, indirect, implied, punitive, special, incidental, or other consequential damages arising directly or indirectly from any use of this work, which is provided as is, without warranties. If you feel you are in crisis, please call the National Suicide Prevention Lifeline. It is a free, 24-hour hotline, at 1-800-273-TALK (8255). Your call will be connected to the crisis center nearest to you. If you are in an emergency, call 911 or go to your nearest emergency room. Dr. Judy Rosenberg and the Psychological Healing Center do not offer emergency services and the information in this book is not intended to be used as such.

ACKNOWLEDGEMENTS

This book is dedicated to my past, present, and future; my dear parents, Susan and Leslie Rosenberg; my wonderful grandparents, Edit and Imre Krausz, and Karolin and Antal Rosenberg for their unconditional love of family and their courage to come to a new country and offer me a life of freedom; my wonderful children Michael and Matthew Perlmutter; my outstanding grandson, Alexander Jonathan Perlmutter, who brings great joy to my life; and to all the wonderful people I have met and yet to meet along my journey—the wisdom masters and friends who will continue to present "curse-by-design" challenges to further my psychospiritual growth. A special thank you to all my staff at the Psychological Healing Center® for helping me create a thriving center for people to come heal. Thank you for all your support in helping to heal Human Disconnect. Thank you to all my patients who have taught me how to be a better psychologist and a better human being. Last of all, thank you Simon, my beautiful canine companion, for your unconditional love and support to all who have come through the doors of the Psychological Healing Center®. And lastly, thank you to my Mind Map™ graphic artist Solomon Augusteyn for creating a beautiful presentation of the many years of my work and helping it all come together.

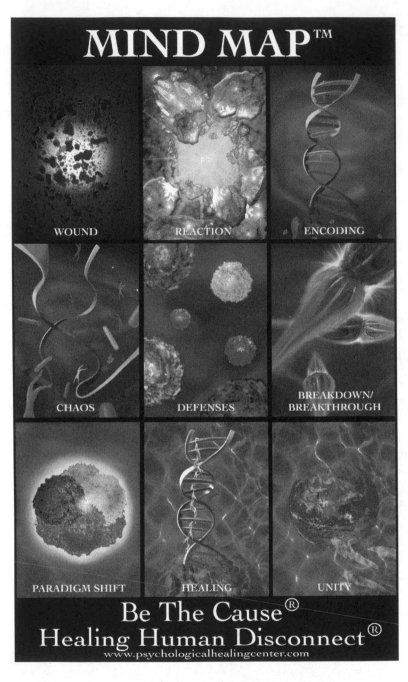

For full color Mind Map, please visit
PsychologicalHealingCenter.com/get-mind-map

PREFACE

"The reason why the world lacks unity and lies broken and in heaps, is because man is disunited with himself."
~ Ralph Waldo Emerson

We are born perfect and connected.

We are then disconnected *from* and made imperfect.

We can become connected and complete again.

YOU can become connected and complete again.

Broken. In heaps. Disunited. Doesn't sound good for the human race, does it? Is this our modern-day fate? A warning? A wake-up call? The great poet Emerson held a mirror up to the human race, and when it reflected back, he did not see a pretty sight. We are a witness to a disconnect between religions, nations, and social classes—a disconnect between mother and child, father and child, husband and wife, our extended families, immediate communities, and the world at large.

Back in 2001, I was having a conversation with a friend about the divided, suffering, self-destructive state of humanity. We spoke of how disconnection between people leads to "*isms*"—oppressive, discriminatory ideologies that fracture our interconnectedness, creating a pathway to annihilation. *Isms* of theology (Catholicism, Judaism, Hinduism, Buddhism, Muslimism, Fundamentalism, etc.) produce exclusionary factions that have the potential to create conflict on a global scale. *Isms* of politics (Capitalism, Socialism, Fascism, etc.) lead to ideological biases that have caused mass destruction. *Isms* of identity (racism, sexism, classism, etc.) promote schisms of ignorance and intolerance that further manifest into prejudice and inequality.

"Isn't it time that we join the human race?" I asked. As these words escaped my lips, the seed of inspiration was born within me. Why not

11

create a system to heal our fractured humanity through healing our fractured sense of self?

With all of our technological advances, it seems that not much has changed in our relationships over the centuries. As a matter of fact, it seems that, as a human race, we have become more disconnected than anytime in recorded history.

After many years of extensive and intensive psychological and spiritual study, I believe I have finally captured, condensed, and abridged decades of theories, case studies, and simple wisdom into an easy-to-use, fast and effective system (my personal $E=MC^2$) for taking any problem in life and converting it into a transformative, paradigm-shifting solution. I call it the **Be The Cause**® System for **Healing Human Disconnect**®.

At the heart of the Be The Cause System is a Mind Map™ matrix, a visual aid to assist you in your journey *From–Through–To*. *From* the problem of disconnect—*through* the dismantling of the **effects** on your mental, emotional, and physical health—*to* a paradigm shift into reconnection and healing.

What I have found time and time again is that the Be The Cause System, coupled with my Mind Map's simplicity and laser-like focus, allows my patients a pathway to heal their mental *dis*-ease much quicker, deeper, and longer lasting than through traditional psychotherapy. I share with you this journey to provide *you* with the same system I share with my patients and provide you comfort and confidence in this extremely effective, proven-in-the-real-world strategy of repair and renewal.

Over the course of your journey, we will look jointly at the **cause** of what I call the **"hole in the soul"**—a sense of emptiness accompanied by symptoms of anxiety and depression brought on by isolation, shame, loneliness, anguish, despair, misery, and other forms of torment. Together we will discover why we became disunited with self.

We will peer into the hole of Human Disconnect, beginning with mother-infant disconnect, and expose the "secret" of how to reverse its effects on our psyche and heart. As we get to the core, or *cause*, of the matter, we will plunge into that chasm like a heat-seeking missile speeding toward its target, unraveling the discordant blueprint of your life and shattering the negative illusions you hold about yourself.

As a psychologist in private practice for over 20 years, I have accumulated a vast body of clinical knowledge and experience alongside over two decades of spiritual study—especially the study of Kabbalah, the secrets of Jewish mysticism. I have found that the inception and strength of the Be The Cause System is rooted in sound psychological theory and ancient Kabbalistic wisdom. Whether you, my dear reader, are atheist, agnostic, or have a belief in God, a higher power, or **Source** (as I like to call it), we can all benefit from diverse common ground teachings that express our need for human interconnectedness, that extol the virtues of loving and being loved unconditionally, and that create a pathway to healing ourselves from the inside out.

Before we can heal globally, we must heal individually and release our suppressed and often painful feelings from the wounds of the past. Ultimately, we must forgive ourselves (and others) by harnessing the most powerful healing force known to man: unconditional love based on principles of truth, integrity, and ethics. I warmly remind you that you are not alone on your journey, that you and I are on this expedition together. Through our intimate and all-embracing collaboration, we will transmute this once life-encompassing trauma of disconnect into reconnection and rebirth of your true, whole, unique, amazing, and soulful self.

Shall we begin?

SETTING YOUR CONSCIOUSNESS

"Control of consciousness determines the quality of life."
~Mihaly Csikszentmihalyi

Max Planck, the father of quantum theory, understood that behind anything that exists there is **consciousness**. It is the organizational concept behind all thoughts, actions, and even the material world as we experience it. He said:

> *I regard consciousness as fundamental. I regard matter as derivative from consciousness. We cannot get behind consciousness. Everything that we talk about, everything that we regard as existing, postulates consciousness.*

We are born. We are wounded. We can heal. You can heal. By setting your intention and/or consciousness now, you can Be The Cause of better outcomes for your life. Consciousness, or intention, is fundamental. Consciousness is causal.

Many of my patients discover that as they shift their consciousness from fragmentation to wholeness, they experience life as more interconnected and "at one." Think of the Mind Map as your $E=MC^2$ quantum, consciousness shifting tool.

The intention behind the Mind Map is to heal the disconnections that wounded you, taking you from the **darkness** of the unconscious to the **light** of the conscious. Think of it as a system that will shift you out of being fragmented and into being whole. For now, take a moment to set your consciousness and/or intention on "healing" and prepare for the first step of your personal Mind Map journey.

INTRODUCTION

"If you can't explain it simply, you don't understand it well enough."
~ Albert Einstein

"You are about to enter another dimension, a dimension not only of sight and sound, but of mind. A journey into a wondrous land of imagination. Next stop..."

You may recognize this narration from the famous Rod Serling TV series, *The Twilight Zone*. I begin with this introduction to acquaint you with a journey into a wondrous new system, a system that offers you a new lens through which to perceive your life, and one that in the beginning may feel "alien" to you. Although change can feel quite strange, let me reassure you that once you learn to adjust your vision and begin perceiving, or "seeing," your world through a new lens, it will seem like a master key is unlocking the mysteries of your unconscious.

I call this new lens, or "psychoperceptual" lens, the Be The Cause System for Healing . Although heredity and organic malfunction can be devastating to the psyche, you will discover through this lens that Human Disconnect is the single most preventable injurious factor to mental health as well as the root cause of inorganic psychopathology, or mental **dis-ease**.

You will also discover that because most genetic attributes cannot be corrected, focusing on the **nurture** aspect of mental *dis*-ease versus the **nature**, or genetic factor, is a more effective approach to the reversal and the healing process. Without this focus on what actually *can* be changed, the hole in the soul will force us to remain unconscious.

At times, I hear words in a piece of music that strike a deep, resonating chord within me. The song *Flaws* by Bastille is one of those songs. I am compelled to share the lyrics with you because they so accurately describe the hole in the soul that generation after generation of Human Disconnect leaves us with:

FLAWS by Bastille

When all of your flaws and all of my flaws

Are laid out one by one

A wonderful part of the mess that we made

We pick ourselves undone

All of your flaws and all of my flaws

They lie there hand in hand

Ones we've inherited, ones that we learned

They pass from man to man

There's a hole in my soul

I can't fill it, I can't fill it

There's a hole in my soul

Can you fill it? Can you fill it?

As we pass down our flaws—person-to-person, generation-to-generation—the hole in the soul grows larger and deeper. Throughout our lives, we attempt to fill this hole with alcohol, drugs, sex, power, money, fame, relationships, and more. But instead of fulfillment, our fruitless attempt to "fill" the hole creates anxiety, depression, isolation, regret, loneliness, anguish, despair, misery, and torment.

As we suffer individually, unable to fill this hole, we inevitably either implode and self-destruct or explode and project our rage and suffering onto others, causing more pain and disconnect. This occurs because we don't know how to cope with the pain and therefore misdirect it at ourselves and/or others.

Through my many explorations, I have discovered time and time again that the origin of inorganic human suffering stems from the earliest detachment in our lives: the mother-infant disconnect. All forms of Human Disconnect have profound negative effects on both our physical and mental well-being. However, none is as profound as the mother-infant and father-infant disconnects.

When we are disconnected *from*, not only do we suffer mentally and emotionally, our bodies undergo painful experiences as our physical health suffers as well. All kinds of somatic symptoms (backaches, headaches, chronic stomach pain, soreness, and much worse) are examples of how intricately the mind and the body are interconnected.

All human beings suffer. It is the nature of life. We all experience suffering in different ways and to different degrees. None of us are immune to life's pain. Some people experience minimal pain and suffering, others undergo much more profound experiences. The case studies presented in this book are based on more extreme examples of pain; however, it is important to know that the Be The Cause Mind Map System is applicable to all cases, both mild and severe.

Sometimes the disconnection in our lives is a result of **acts of commission**, or what is done *to* us. Overt examples of commission are physical abuse, sexual abuse, or verbal abuse—such as being criticized, shamed, blamed, or judged. An often overlooked form of overt abuse is emotional smothering, often mistaken for love and care.

Sometimes disconnection results from covert actions, or **acts of omission**. This type of disconnect reflects what was not done *for* us. Emotional or physical neglect—beginning in infancy and early childhood— are prime examples of acts of omission.

Often, acts of omission or neglect can seem even more painful than overt abuse to the person on the receiving end. One of my patients reported that, at age four, she put her hand on a hot stove just to get her parents' attention. Some of us would rather suffer excruciating pain than be ignored or disconnected from.

British psychiatrist and psychoanalyst John Bowlby, father of **attachment theory,** and his colleague, American-Canadian developmental psychologist Mary Ainsworth, did massive research on the effects of maternal deprivation on infants and young children separated from their mother or primary caregiver. Their work with delinquent children deprived of affection and the effects of hospital and institutional care led to Bowlby being commissioned to write the World Health Organization's 1952 Geneva report on the mental health of homeless children in post-war Europe.

Back in the 1950s in Europe, the relationship between mother and infant as a factor in healthy child development was an unheard of concept. It was Bowlby who stated: "The infant and young child should experience a warm, intimate, and continuous relationship with his mother (or permanent mother-substitute) in which both find satisfaction and enjoyment."

Bowlby went on to explain that without this type of attuned, love-centered bonding, significant and irreversible mental health consequences would occur. In laymen's terms, what Bowlby was stating was that an integrally significant factor in healthy development is the power of unconditional love in the form of selfless, infant-child centered parenting.

In Bowlby's own childhood, he typically saw his mother only one hour a day. Like many other mothers of the upper-middle-class British, she believed that parental attention and affection would lead to dangerous spoiling of the child.

Raised by a nanny who left the family when he was almost four years old, Bowlby described her departure as akin to the loss of a mother. Evidently, this was the wound that fueled his interest in attachment theory. Some of my own wounds of childhood have subsequently fueled my interest in his attachment theory as well.

Because Bowlby so elegantly explains the hole in the soul phenomenon from a psychological perspective, I acknowledge and continue to honor his work through my Be The Cause System for Healing Human Disconnect. The fact that he was so "spot on" at a time when the rest of society felt the opposite makes me admire him that much more.

Although Bowlby never defined attachment theory in terms of unconditional love per se there was no psychoanalyst more attuned to the effects of the lack of unconditional love on mental health. His research confirmed that mother-infant disconnect has a devastating effect on the human psyche.

I will refer to Bowlby and his attachment theory often in this book as we go on this journey together. It is one of the key theories that I have built my Be The Cause System upon. It is my hope that you will see his brilliant work woven into all that you are about to learn in the coming Panels.

Whether we view Human Disconnect through the microcosmic lens of mother-infant disconnect or through the macrocosmic lens of global disconnect, the same theme appears. The hole in the soul within each of us can only be filled with the most powerful healing force in the universe: unconditional love.

By coloring outside-of-the-lines of my profession and immersing myself in spiritual wisdom and studies, I am convinced that the power of unconditional love—a subject not talked about enough in the profession of psychology—is a crucial and causal aspect of healing. Through self-love—and by extending it to family, friends, and community—we can all become agents of healing.

Whether you believe in Source, nature, universal intelligence, universal truth, or God, we can all agree on some basic universal truths: unconditional love is a powerful healing force. Self-expression (not repression) of our deepest authenticity is a healthy way to prevent the emotional implosions and explosions that detonate our hopes, dreams, and ultimately, our mental health. Judging, blaming, shaming, and criticizing are forms of harming the self and others, while **self-reflecting** to **self-correct** is a pathway to evolving.

The reason I call my system the Be The Cause System for Healing Human Disconnect is two-fold: Human Disconnect, as explained above, is the source of untold human suffering; second, you are going to be learning a system that teaches you to Be The Cause of the experiences and outcomes in your life by setting your "consciousness" or intention (where we are "coming from" you might say) on principles that serve you and others best.

For example, when we come from a consciousness of judgment, criticism, hate, negative intention, or shame, we attract, reinforce, and create more darkness in our lives. Conversely, if we come from a consciousness of non-judgment, cooperation, love, compassion, and hope, we invite strength and growth into our lives. As you learn to see the world through the lens of your new consciousness, you will learn to be the master of creating better outcomes for your life.

As Albert Einstein says, "You cannot solve a problem from the same consciousness that created it. You must learn to see the world anew." However you want to look at it, new, healthier patterns have to be learned in order to grow beyond (and eventually replace) the old, obsolete, destructive patterns.

The heart intention behind the Be The Cause System is to create a pathway to reconnection and healing—*from* the wounds of disconnect; *through* the dismantling of the effects of these wounds on your psyche and overall health; *to* paradigm shifting into interconnection, reconnection, and unity. As you learn to dismantle the old, encoded misinformation and recode into health, you will ultimately learn to Be The Cause of far better outcomes for your life.

Although we are going to explore the ways in which we have been wounded (through no fault of our own), we are also going to take full responsibility for our lives by doing the work it takes to liberate ourselves from the suffering of the past. We cannot change the negative experiences of the past, but we can change our perception of them and diminish their dark power over us through the shifting of our consciousness. By learning to view every event through a perspective of connection/disconnection, you will see that this game of light versus darkness is about recognizing the wounds, exploring and dismantling their effects on you, and learning to reconnect and "reboot" your entire **system gone wrong**.

At the heart of my Be The Cause System is the Mind Map, a nine Panel visual matrix of information rich in metaphor. It is my personal paradigm shifting $E=MC^2$ formula for healing. The Mind Map will teach you how to actively direct your consciousness to get the results you intend.

You will learn, using the practical and straightforward imagery of the Mind Map, how the initial disconnect in your life (with your birth mother or primary caregiver), coupled with other early parental detachments and deficiencies, created the blueprint of **negative core beliefs** about who you are and what you think, feel, accept, and believe about yourself.

These negative core beliefs—interwoven into the fiber of your being during the formative years of your life, beginning at the preverbal (before language) stage of infancy—become the unconscious (and later, more conscious) foundation of your self-identity. Everything that you experience through the perceptual lens of your core beliefs becomes your perception of who you *believe* you are.

For most of us, our primary core belief is profoundly negative: *"I am not good enough. I am unlovable. I am worthless. I am not important enough to be number one,"* or some other similar, self-disparaging variation. Once this negative core belief gets entrenched in our psyche (I like to think of it as a "psychological virus," or **"psycho-virus"**—the type that makes you psycho), it infects our self-perception and forms the basis of our inherent insecurities and self-unacceptance. As we *ingest* and *digest* our negative core beliefs, we *manifest* them in our relationships with ourselves and others. This primary negative core belief—our psychological "Achilles' heel"— and the offshoot negative core beliefs get retriggered when we judge ourselves, when we feel judged and/or criticized by others, or any time our feelings get hurt.

Once "infected" with this negative core belief, we begin to look for proof from the world around us to reinforce our concept of self-worthlessness. Everything in our lives that scares us, undermines us, depresses us, sabotages us, numbs us, tortures us, threatens us, oppresses us, etc., is based on the content and potency of this negative core belief.

Once you begin to see the potentially cataclysmic consequences of your present-day view of yourself and the world as seen through the lens of your negative core belief, you will appreciate how important it is to do the work to dismantle it. As you break apart this negative core belief, you will debilitate its power over you and allow the intentional forces of your consciousness to direct your life.

One of the great injustices—perhaps just as woeful as any of our suffering—is the fact that we see ourselves through this cracked and distorted lens of disparaging self-worth, and then blame ourselves for the so-called "failure" of our lives. But the truth is, none of it is our fault. We are not the genesis of this negative core belief from childhood, just as we are not the cause of **Part One of our lives**. Take it in and contemplate it for a moment. You are not the cause of ingesting this negative core belief and allowing it to infiltrate into the core of your being. None of the information that created the blueprint of your core belief has to do with you. None.

Helpless and completely dependent upon our caregivers for sustenance, safety, security, nurturing, and unconditional love, we depended on them for our self-definition. If we were lucky enough to have parents that were emotionally mature and dedicated, and present enough to attune to our needs, we were blessed. But the majority of us were not.

Let me be perfectly clear: this system is not a system of blaming, shaming, criticizing, or judging our parents (or ourselves if we are parents). It is a system based on allowing ourselves to cleanse the wounds of our past, preventing ourselves from creating future wounds in our next generation, and ultimately forgiving ourselves and our parents for their and our human flaws. It is a system based on an understanding that these wounds are multigenerational, that our parents are not the cause of Part One of their lives either.

Most of us experienced covert, subtle forms of abuse from our caregivers (lack of attunement, disconnection, self-absorption). Others were subject to more overt forms (physical, verbal, or sexual abuse). Powerless to shield ourselves from these intrusions to our psyche, these undesirable influences enter our minds and marrow without any buffer. We ingested them because we were emotionally permeable sponges, ready to receive what was encoded into us, allowing it to mold our developing personalities, attitudes, and values.

In the course of your Mind Map journey, you will learn that we are hostages and casualties of childhood. Up until now, we have been unable to fully identify, hold responsible, and ultimately forgive the injurers—our parents.

To add further insult to considerable injury, nearly all of the cues, intuitions, and information that we unconsciously "sopped up like a biscuit" and used to form our negative core beliefs are based on lies, falsehoods, and fabrications, usually based on our parents' own negative core beliefs from their childhoods. The inheritances that our parents gave us beyond genetics were the hand-me-downs of suppression, neglect, and maltreatment from their own difficult upbringings.

This is a multigenerational virus that keeps on giving, right on down the line. Inevitably, this replication, if not disrupted and transmuted, will germinate, and these psycho-viruses will infect the next generation, passing down to our children the childhood wounds passed down to us.

The Be The Cause System was created for you and future generations. Through a deeper understanding (and subsequent cleansing) of the complexities, breadth, and intensity of the profound wounds of childhood, we can stop this horrific process from transmitting to the next generation and truly "going viral."

As we move away from the superficial cognitive and/or behavior modification and medication management treatment plans and look at the *cause* of the wound, we can begin to realize that simply "modifying" or numbing out our own and our children's pain is antithetical to healing. Although I myself use these adjunctive tools and treatments in my practice, they are never a substitute for a treatment plan based on looking into and treating the originating cause.

As we move away from blaming, shaming, judging, and criticizing ourselves for the not-so-ideal outcome of Part One of our lives, we will no longer simply settle for glossing over our parents' personal responsibilities for creating our state of *dis*-ease. As we begin to understand the multigenerational nature of psychopathology (and the need to heal ourselves before we take on the responsibility of becoming parents), we can finally hold our parents therapeutically responsible and accountable for passing down the impact of their unhealed wounds. Only then can we begin to heal the wounds presently festering in our (and our children's) bodies, hearts, and minds.

As we move toward healing at the *causal* level, we can head towards deep, sustainable restoration and stop this multigenerational transmission of pathology that leaves us all highly susceptible to suffering and disease later in life. This interruption of the process is one of the most pleasurable and rewarding aspects of my work. I call it "healing forward."

The Mind Map is a very easy and powerful visual tool for illuminating how the wounds of childhood were delivered and embedded, and how they have manifested into your life. It is an active instrument that creates a pathway out of the symptoms and into the work of healing, and incorporates a matrix full of empowering information and metaphors. It is based on a *from-through-to* model: *from* the problem (or creation/encoding of the problem), *through* the process (or dismantling/decoding of the problem), and *to* the solution (or paradigm shift and recoding into solution).

THE MIND MAP EXPLAINED

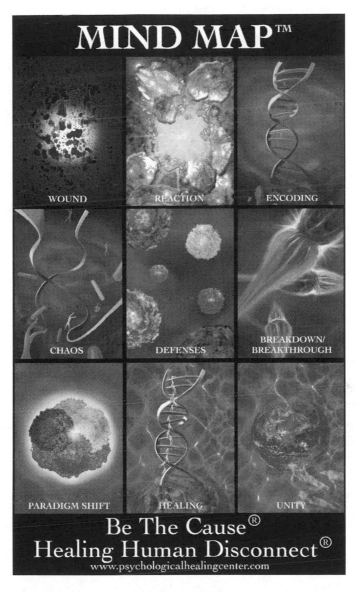

Please look closely at the Mind Map. There are nine Panels. They are organized into three rows of three, from left to right and top to bottom. The top row (Panels One, Two, and Three) deals with Creation/Encoding—Your Past. The middle row (Four, Five, and Six) focuses on Destruction/Decoding—Your Present. The bottom row (Seven, Eight, and Nine) explores Reintegration/Recoding—Your Future.

With this clear-cut structure, the Mind Map is designed to mimic the natural flow of life: from birth to death to rebirth. Just as life is created from an original cause, broken apart, destroyed, and then reorganized into higher forms, problems too can be seen as created, dismantled, and reintegrated *from* the problem (Row One), *through* the process (Row Two), and *to* the solution (Row Three). The graphics are vivid and simple, allowing people of all ages and cultures to grasp the concepts intuitively and understand the logic, symbolism, metaphors, and problem-solving attributes of the Mind Map™ quickly. This formidable tool will allow you to transform your own deep-rooted issues and challenges into conscious, creative solutions. Ultimately, the Mind Map™ is a visual representation of a system designed to prevent problems before they begin. As Albert Einstein once said, "Intellectuals solve problems. Geniuses prevent them."

Now that you understand the basic structure of the Mind Map, let us get a little more specific about what each panel represents in the progression of our lives.

CREATION: *FROM* THE PROBLEM
Encoding—Your Past.

PANEL ONE represents the *Wound*, the original disconnect between mother and infant. On the Mind Map, it is represented by an image of the Big Bang, or "First Cause." This is the first representation of duality (our darkness and our light) and the introduction into the psyche of first needs unfulfilled, first struggles and disappointments, and first sensations of self and others.

PANEL TWO represents the *Reaction* to the Wound. Primitive emotional experiences centered around comfort/discomfort and pleasure/pain begin to form. The amygdala—the primitive part of our brain responsible for emotions like fear and anger—encodes both soothing (connecting) experiences and traumatic (disconnecting) experiences. When disconnected *from*, the infant reacts *to* the wounds of disconnect by crying or shutting down. In early infant development, these reactions are preverbal—before words, thoughts, or cognitions. As the infant develops, the self acquires and shapes feelings into thoughts. Over time, the mind absorbs, clutches, and creates meaning through experiences. Life becomes more intricate and potentially more dangerous.

PANEL THREE represents the *Encoding* of the Wound. Cognitions, thoughts, feelings, emotions, and behaviors become patterns encoded into our being, creating an unconscious blueprint or negative core belief that manifests into our relationship with ourselves, others, and with the world around us. This encoding comes from our parents' messages, their treatment of us (encoded when we were in the preverbal stage of development), and the words they spoke (encoded when we were in the verbal stages of development) that we have claimed as our own.

More often than not, this encoding is painfully negative, leaving us with a reproachful self-perception based on the lies "infiltrated" into our consciousness. These infiltrations, or psycho-viruses, later crystallize and inevitably become our negative core beliefs. We combine the many voices of judgment and disparagement—now firmly implanted in our heads— into one voice of self-critical disapproval. It is then through this dark, cracked lens that we perceive ourselves and the world.

Then, unconsciously, we begin to look for "proof" that confirms our self-judgment by projecting our false interpretations onto the world, whether they fit in reality or not. This reinforces our self-crimination deeper into our psyche. Think of it as the world mirroring back to us how we feel about ourselves.

The world, now merely a mirror reflecting back the lies we have taken as truth, becomes an unsafe place to live in. Soon, these triggered feelings catapult us into the abyss of chaos. I call it the beginning of the formation of the "**double dungeon of darkness**"—darkness from within and darkness from without. Trapped in a double dungeon of darkness, we feel imprisoned and hopeless, turning deeper inward into isolation and self-reproach.

DESTRUCTION: *THROUGH* THE PROCESS
Decoding—Your Present.

PANEL FOUR represents *Chaos*. It manifests when others reinjure our initial wounds. Think of these reinjuries as triggers that activate our negative core belief(s). The undercurrent of ambiguity and uncertainty that begins at the preverbal infant stage, combined with our inexplicable sense of being disconnected, breaks us down into profound anxiety, cynicism, and hopelessness.

As we further implode or project these fears onto others, the resulting chaos forces us to look for ways to cope with the anguish and agony of our despair, including wearing rose colored glasses and using quick fix techniques to deny the problems at hand.

PANEL FIVE represents *Defense Mechanisms*. In order to deal with the heavy burden of chaos and suffering imposed on us by our negative core beliefs, we begin to generate defense mechanisms—methods of rationalization, deflection, and avoidance to brace against the fear of letting go of the problem or issue. This only serves to exacerbate the problem over time. Eventually, we become unwavering, impervious, and brittle in order to block out our own poisoning self-image and life's confirmation of it.

But sadly, our impermeable shield also blocks out the light of emotional nourishment. As we cautiously attempt to let in some sun, we often overcompensate, tipping the scales in the opposite direction. We become porous, allowing toxins to infiltrate and injure our vulnerable, disjointed psyche. Because of this, we suffer, be it by poisoning, starvation, or putting our heads in the sand and delaying the inevitable.

PANEL SIX represents the *Breakdown/Breakthrough* of unhealthy and unsustainable defense mechanisms that no longer function to help you manage your life. In extreme cases, the war within us reaches a climax— exploding into aggression/hostility or imploding into depression/anxiety—leaving us (and those around us) shattered, traumatized, and in turmoil. Breakdown/Breakthrough occurs when we reach **critical mass**, the tipping point between destruction and rebirth. It is at this tipping point that the walls crumble around us, and we are left holding the remnants in our hands. What we do from this point forward forecasts our fate and decides our destiny.

REINTEGRATION: *TO* THE SOLUTION
Recoding—Your Future.

PANEL SEVEN represents the *Paradigm Shift*. A paradigm shift is a new way of *seeing* yourself and the world around you and a new way of *being* or relating to yourself and the world around you. As you begin to clear up your cracked lens of psychoperception, you will learn to direct your consciousness with intention, put an end to being at the *effect* of life, and learn to Be The *Cause*.

PANEL EIGHT represents *Healing*. Once limiting core beliefs dismantle, the old, infected DNA blueprint can dismantle, atrophy, and die, allowing you to reboot your system and begin the process of healing and recoding. By encoding healthier thoughts, behaviors, and habits into the fiber of your being, you can create a hardier, more sustainable sense of self. By sharing your health and linking up with like-minded people on the same DNA pathway to healing, you can blueprint an evolving synergistic system for yourself and others, as well as for the next generation.

PANEL NINE represents *Unity*. Living in unity creates a radical shift in the way you live your life. It is a new way of relating to yourself, your immediate community, and the world at large. When you are in unity with yourself, you can begin to manifest all your hopes, dreams, and aspirations and become a trailblazer to others. When in unity, the entire planet (including our animals and the ecosystem) benefits.

The Mind Map is a very easy-to-use and powerful tool to illustrate how the wounds of childhood were delivered, embedded, and manifested into present day life. The Mind Map will help you understand, track, and dismantle a *system gone wrong.* As you will see, it elucidates exactly what is necessary to paradigm shift out of the wounds of childhood and into a healthier, more sustainable system.

Are you still with me? Good. It gets more interesting once we break it all down in the coming Panels.

To summarize the domino effect of this process by Panels:

1.   Problem begins.

2.   Problem manifests into feelings/thoughts/behaviors.

3.   Problem becomes encoded into your psyche, creating patterns.

4.   Problem causes massive breakdown/confusion or chaos.

5.   Problem comes up against resistance or defenses.

6.   Problem comes to a head, imploding/exploding, causing more chaos or new opportunity to decode the old.

7.   Problem paradigm shifts into a new and sustainable system.

8.   New, positive solutions encode into your being, allowing healing in our relationships with self and others.

9.   The new personal consciousness spreads to a positive world consciousness, ultimately leading you back to unity with yourself and all of life.

Simple as pie (or pi as mathematicians like to say!). The Mind Map offers nine slices of exploring your life through a kaleidoscope of systems, patterns, new perceptions, ideas, and challenges in a way that is thought-provoking, intimate, amusing, and—most of all—effective.

At times, I will make connections between the Be The Cause journey and my favorite childhood book and film, *The Wizard of Oz* by Frank L. Baum. *The Wizard of Oz* is a perfect allegory to describe the yellow-brick-road journey to self-knowledge, a journey far outside the box of traditional psychotherapeutic interventions.

The mythology of *The Wizard of Oz,* not unlike the Be The Cause Mind Map, is replete with vivid visuals and metaphorical mirrors, symbols that act upon our psyche and create gateways into our unconscious. These doorways allow us to reflect upon our deepest concept of self and our relationship to the universe.

Along the journey, you get to discover, explore, and unravel the internal and external mysteries of existence and the meanings that you assign to them in your own life. As it has been said, "The road to Oz is the road to self-knowledge." Einstein once remarked, "Imagination is more important than knowledge. Knowledge is limited. Imagination encircles the world."

In the course of your process, I will teach you how to "**think like a shrink**" so that you can connect the dots of disconnection and move your life forward. By laying down logical tracks, your emotions can begin to trust your logic and flow along these tracks.

There will never be a better time for you to use your logic and newly acquired consciousness to challenge your false beliefs in order to find your truest self. There will never be a better time to explore the promise that shifting your consciousness holds for you. And there will never be a better time to regain your equilibrium.

So, I invite you now to turn the page, open up to new possibilities, and get ready to Be The Cause of creating better outcomes for your life!

PANEL ONE

FROM THE PROBLEM: ENCODING

WOUND

"The wound is the place where the Light enters you."
~ Rumi

Whatever begins to exist has a cause. At its core, the Be The Cause System recognizes that there is a beginning, or *cause*, to all things, and specifically, a cause to our deep-rooted and underlying issues. When I question existence, I prefer to focus on the original cause.

Although the Be The Cause System was inspired by my studies of psychology, spirituality, biology, and the Big Bang theory of creation, the focus of this book is to look deeply into the first cause of mental disease, or as I like to call it, mental *dis*-ease, and trace our symptoms back to it.

The heart of this system is based on a psychospiritual and psychological foundation. I assure you that this is not a "religious" model. There is no dogma, no rules, no regulations or "commandments" to follow, and no sins to repent. Let us look further into the cause.

Neurobiological findings substantiate that infant/child abuse and neglect is traumatically injurious to the psyche. According to Danya Glaser, M.D., a psychiatrist from the University College, London, the trauma of abuse and neglect not only interferes with our emotional development but interferes with our cognitive and physical development as well. According to Glaser:

It has been shown that there are considerable changes in brain structure and function in association with both traumatic abuse and severe neglect. The fact that many of these changes are related to aspects of the stress response is not surprising. Because brain development highly depends on the infant's early experiences, these new neurobiological findings shed some light on the many emotional and

31

behavioral difficulties abused and neglected children exhibit over time. We now better understand issues such as hyper-arousal, aggressive responses, dissociative reactions, difficulties with aspects of executive functions and educational underachievement.

I stand witness to these findings. Based on over 20 years of working with patients, it is my opinion that mother-infant disconnect and father-infant disconnect (or disconnection from the primary caregiver), in the form of neglect and abuse, is the first cause (or root cause) of preventable, inorganic psychopathology, cognitive impairment, and psychosomatic illness.

It is sad (yet not uncommon) that the very caregivers who were meant to protect and love us unconditionally fail to provide their infants and children with the emotional ingredients that create a healthy human psyche. Worse, many times these same caregivers don't want to take the time to self-reflect, self-correct, and heal their emotional wounds themselves so that they can offer their children better parenting.

Whether the inability to provide "good enough" parenting was intentional or unintentional—nature does not care—the effects are the same. For the time being, we will disregard the reasons so we can focus on the cause and dismantle the effects.

Children are not born with a care manual, and parents, for the most part, don't possess the skills and education for how to parent, as their parents most likely didn't teach them. Worse yet, many parents rely on "experts" who sometimes misinform. In the following chapters, you will learn much about the injurious effects of Human Disconnect on the psyche and learn how to break out of the multigenerational prison of hand-me-down psychopathology.

FROM WOMB TO WOUND

"The neglect and humiliation of a child by adults is a killer of trust, of hope, and of possibility...Is there anything more important than a child? Is there? Is there another time in your life when love, care, tenderness, food, education are more important than in a childhood?"
~Audrey Hepburn

Childhood is a hostage situation. We have no control over the way our caregivers parent us (or fail to). As infants and children, we are in their hands, for better or for worse. If we are fortunate, our parents provide us with safety, nurturance, and attunement—all expressions of unconditional love. Some parents—usually because they received "good enough" parenting themselves—have a lot of light to give. Other parents—usually because they didn't receive good enough parenting—have little to give and cast a shadow over our sense of well-being.

From the first moment of birth we are expelled into the world. The umbilical cord is cut, we take our first gasp of air, and we leave the comfort zone of the womb. Birth is our first experience of mother-infant disconnect.

Life consists of a series of necessary separations. Healthy separations foster growth and help us separate, individuate, mature, and evolve. However, not all separations are created equal. While it is inevitable that at times our primary caregiver will fail to attend to our needs quickly enough, it is the harmful separations of abuse and neglect that leave us emotionally compromised, crippled, and/or unable to grow and flourish.

An often overlooked injury to the psyche is the injurious effects of being "smothered." Some parents are so overprotective that they don't allow their infant/child to properly separate and individuate, instead keeping them imprisoned in dependency. This type of injury can be just as crippling to growth and development as abuse and neglect. The "helicopter parent," or hovering parent, a concept you may be familiar with, is a prime example of emotional smothering.

Please recall that the wounds inflicted on you during Part One (your infancy and childhood) were not caused by you and are not your fault. You are not the cause of Part One of your life. You are not the cause of what happened to you in your first few years of life.

As infants and children, we are at the effect versus at the cause of our life. Because we were unable to control what happened to us, and worse, because we were unable to express and communicate our pain to the very people who caused us pain, these injuries got stored in our minds and bodies in the form of emotional and physical symptoms. The mind and body are intricately connected, so when we hurt emotionally, we hurt physically, and vice versa.

Symptoms are the language of the unconscious. When the wounds of our past cannot be expressed and processed emotionally, they manifest as symptoms. When we repress our feelings, we either turn them inward, and against ourselves, or project them onto others.

Symptoms of repression can manifest as depression, a result of anger turned inward. At times symptoms of repression manifest somatically as backaches, headaches, or stomach aches—the mind and the body are interconnected.

Symptoms of aggression, on the other hand, are the result of anger turned outward. Symptoms of aggression manifest as acting out on others—yelling and/or hitting or physically harming others, for example.

The more we repress or aggress, the more we thwart authentic expression and healing. You will learn more about the insidious process of repression and aggression and how they stunt our psychological growth.

Unable to stay silent, our symptoms, like writing-on-the-wall clues or hieroglyphics, continue to "talk" to us, and even escalate and "yell" at us, until we decide to address them. As you learn to *think like a shrink*, you will learn to decipher the clues and connect the dots that point an arrow back to the cause of the symptoms, allowing you to finally address the repressed pain and finish your psychological business.

When we suppress the expression of our authentic feelings and silence our "bad" ones to protect our caregivers and/or protect ourselves from our caregivers, when we project our anger onto others to avoid the anger we feel towards the "original cause," we pay a huge emotional price. As children we are unable (and unsafe) to know what the truth is and how to say it to the people who hurt us (usually our primary caregivers), so we stay silent or redirect the pain. The fear of retribution and rejection stops us from speaking out. After all, we "can't bite the hand that feeds us."

Many of my patients have undergone unconscionable maltreatment by their caregivers and have had to suppress their authentic, hurt, angry, taboo feelings for fear of retribution and rejection, or just because they didn't know that what was happening to them was not their fault. When we turn those feelings inward or project them outward, we become emotionally sick and/or contaminate others with our pain. When we express, we begin to heal. Far too often, people don't ask for help until they are brought to their proverbial knees by the intolerable pain of their symptoms. This is usually when I get a call for help.

In her brilliant book, *Prisoners of Childhood: The Drama of the Gifted Child and the Search for the True Self,* psychoanalyst Alice Miller talks about how repressing our true authentic feelings create a "false (repressed) self." Not safe to say the truth about how we feel, we blame ourselves for the bad around us. Alice Miller says, "a child would rather be a bad child in a good world than a good child in a bad world," meaning that children would rather blame themselves (and think they are at fault) than think that they are living in a bad and unsafe world.

I remind you again: You are not the cause of Part One of your life. You are not the cause of what happened to you in your first few years of your life. You are not the cause of your mental pain and suffering!

As an adult, you are no longer hostage to your childhood. Although you may find that you are still mentally hostage to your past, you are now free to choose to take a journey out of your darkness of repression and into the light of self-expression, so that you can learn how to Be The Cause of **Part Two of your life**.

THE PATHWAY TO HEALING

The pathway to healing is a non-judgmental pathway with truth as your guiding light. As you begin to therapeutically express your taboo feelings, you will begin to correct your cracked lens of psychoperception and begin to decipher the lies from the truth. The truth process is not a blame, shame, or "throw your parents under the bus" plan. And, in case you were wondering, there is no need to hurt your parents in the process. No parent has been harmed by the healing process, and most of the time, they are not present to your **"truth conversations"**—therapeutic conversations meant to express repressed emotions.

Some parents opt to participate in the healing process with their children. When they do, it is often as life changing and healing for them as it is for their children. It is an honor for me to do this type of multigenerational work. I call it **"healing backwards"** because I am helping the parent(s) heal their wounds as well.

As you journey *from-through-to*, I suggest that you pack lightly. You will need:

- A Truth Light to **Self-Reflect**. Carry it with you at all times, and feel free to shine it on the dark repressed areas of your past. As you begin to expose the wounds that infiltrated into the fiber of your being, use the truth light to illuminate and dissolve any unconscious lies that limit or have limited your growth. Recall that darkness cannot exist in the presence of light—no matter how dim.

- A Mirror to **Self-Correct**. As you learn to look at the harmful thoughts, feelings, and behaviors that have penetrated and encoded into your psyche, you can begin to self-correct and break free from being a hostage to your past. I suggest you use your mirror to self-reflect on who you are becoming as you self-correct and recode into your authentic self.

- Self-Acceptance. As you learn to put your relationship with yourself as primary and learn to love and accept yourself, you will begin to understand the powerful healing force of unconditional love. As you let go of judging, blaming, shaming, and criticizing yourself, you may find that your mental health, your ethics, and your treatment of others improves as well.

What you need to leave behind: judgment, shame, blame, and self-criticism. Stay clear of these negative forms of consciousness as they will only trip you up, land you into the chasm of darkness, and thwart your journey.

As you travel along the yellow-brick-road to healing, you may need to leave your comfort zone. As you eventually make a paradigm shift out of your "old" self and into the new, you may find that you may become unrecognizable to yourself and others. No need to panic: It's by your own free choice.

THE "CURSE-BY-DESIGN" GIFT

M. Scott Peck M.D., in his timeless and insightful book, *The Road Less Traveled: A New Psychology of Love* talked about suffering:

> *To proceed very far from the desert, you must be willing to meet existential suffering and work it through. In order to do this, the attitude toward pain has to change. This happens when we accept that everything that happens to us has been designed for our spiritual growth.*

Dr. Peck's quote describes what I call the "**curse-by-design**," a concept that I will be referring to frequently. The curse-by-design concept is a way to regard the sacredness of the wounds from our past as an opportunity to help us grow emotionally and spiritually. To move forward in our lives with wisdom, courage, and compassion, we must embrace and accept our curse-by-design, allowing it to shatter the un-truths of our past, and shift our perception from illusion to truth.

According to ancient spiritual teachings, darkness is the absence of light. When the veil of darkness is lifted, there exists only unconditional love. Ancient spiritual texts and religious mysticism all support this prevailing, life-affirming notion.

What does it all mean? In order to truly heal our wounds, truly forgive our parents (and ourselves), and flourish in this enormous and often difficult world, we must enter our dark, infiltrated past and finally come face-to-face with the lies and misinformation we encoded into our being—starting at the *causal* level.

As we expunge the poison of our infiltrated past, we have a new opportunity to dismantle the old blueprint, recode the future, and pay our mental health forward to our future generations. I call this entire process—"healing the past," "healing the now," and "healing the future"—"**healing forward**."

As you absorb the information in this book, think of all your wounds from your past as your curse-by-design injuries that have left a gaping hole in your soul to, as the philosopher Rumi says, "allow the light to enter you." They are designed to help you grow psychologically and spiritually if you permit them to be your teacher and impart more wisdom into your life.

Notice the light in Panel One on the next page. The light is a symbol of your healthy, ongoing struggle to break through the darkness of your unconscious and end the cycle of pain and suffering that poisons you from the inside out. The light also represents your conscious and healthy manifestation of your whole, complete, authentic self, which I will be referring to as your "**Big *I***."

The darkness, on the other hand, is a symbol of your unconscious, unhealthy, injured, compromised, un-manifested self, yearning to heal and transform. I will be referring to the darkness as your "**Little *I***." Look again at Panel One. Like an enormous sun obstructed by sunspots, the giant, occluded eye represents your mother's multigenerational hauntings and her resultant compromised sense of self-worth. These shadows represent the break in eye-to-eye contact between you and your mother, creating the mother-infant disconnect.

PANEL ONE: A VISUAL METAPHOR
FOR YOUR UNCONSCIOUS WOUNDS

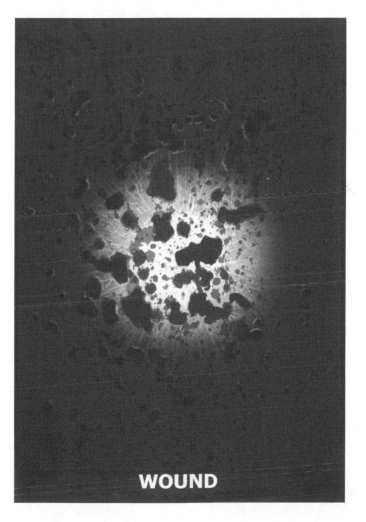

WOUND

"Until you make the unconscious conscious, it will direct your life
and you will call it fate." ~ C.G. Jung

When we are disconnected from, we become emotionally vulnerable to being infiltrated by psychological viruses, or psycho-viruses. They attack our sense of emerging self and leave us feeling "psycho," or crazy. These psycho-viruses, a term I will be referring to frequently, are like cruel and dangerous adversaries that invade and attack our sense of self, health, and well-being.

Not unlike physical viruses that seek to destroy the body's defense system, these psycho-viruses act like an army, assaulting the stronghold of your self-concept and slaughtering it with every means in its arsenal—lies, fabrications, half-truths, misrepresentations, deceptions, and myths.

Feeding off of your deeply rooted feelings of neglect, deprivation, and abuse, these mercenary psycho-viruses have but one mission: to annihilate your sense of self-worth and leave a gaping hole in the soul where joy once lived. Once infiltrated with these psycho-viruses, they take over and replicate their psycho-DNA into the fiber of your being.

The hole in the soul is that torturous emptiness and self-loathing buried in the depths of our being. Like a malignant tumor, it is fed and fueled by Human Disconnect, the basis of preventable inorganic psychopathology. The yearning and longing for connection to self and others, wired deep within us, remains unquenched, leaving us feeling abandoned, starved, and forsaken.

EMOTIONAL INGREDIENTS FOR MENTAL HEALTH

You could say that the very nature of life itself is a process of separation, an inherent and necessary part of life. Think of the birthing process: contractions—nature's way of removing us from the comfort zone of the womb; the cutting of the umbilical cord—our first experience of separation from mother.

Life consists of a series of necessary separations—separations that foster growth, that cause us to evolve. Recall that not all separations are created equal. The unnecessary, wayward separations create wounds to the self. When parents fail to soften the disconnect by not attuning to their children, a secure base for healthy development cannot be established.

Post-birth, the primary needs of the newborn infant are nearly absolute. The infant's basic physiological needs (breast milk, food, warmth, shelter) are just part of their requirements for optimal health. According to Bowlby's attachment theory, interactions between mother and infant—from birth through the first two to three years of life—are paramount for bonding. Proximity, touch, eye contact, breastfeeding, emotional nourishment, expressions of love, etc., all have a profound impact on healthy development. Their interruption or absence can set all kinds of negative consequences into motion.

Put simply, you gazed into the eyes of your mother to "see" your value. If she gazed back lovingly and attentively on a consistent basis throughout your infancy, you were fortunate enough to receive the right ingredients necessary for healthy human emotional development. This attunement allowed you to feel safe and cared for, forming the foundation of your emotional well-being. This unconditional love, based on attunement, reinforced and preserved the light you entered the world with, allowing you to explore and flourish.

On the other hand, if you were ignored, injured, or deprived of touch, eye contact, or consistent love and attention, the dark, infiltrated (wounded) eyes of your primary caregiver, devoid of the light of unconditional love, reflected back negatively on you, reinforcing your lack of value. From one generation to the next, these psycho-viruses cast a shadow over our caregivers, blocking their ability to parent selflessly by putting the needs of the infant/child first. The result is an epidemic of depression, anxiety, and despair, in addition to other preventable, inorganic psychopathology present in the human condition.

THE PREEMIE PROBLEM

Incubator babies, or "preemies," are perhaps the most obvious and dramatic example of how Human Disconnect between mother and infant can cause a myriad of negative consequences. Doctors have long studied the physical symptoms of premature infants who do not receive enough touch—coordination problems, language deficiencies, difficulty with memory and reading, behavioral issues (such as overly aggressive play or excessive loudness), visual impairments, dental decay, weakened immunity, respiratory concerns, and increased risk of death are examples of symptoms of touch-deprived infants.

If these indicators aren't terrifying enough, we are now learning that mental ailments such as psychosis, depression, and bipolar disorder often follow the newborn into childhood, adolescence, and adulthood. Recent brain research indicates that the neural pathways of the brain are altered when we are disconnected *from*, and conversely, positively altered when we are emotionally connected *to*.

According to Allan Schore, M.D., a leading researcher in the field of neuropsychology, "...the overwhelming stress of maltreatment (abuse and neglect) is associated with adverse influences on brain development." Dr. Schore points to "relational trauma" as having a bigger impact on the developing infant brain than physical trauma from the environment.

He further concludes that a dysfunctional early relationship can lead to Post-Traumatic Stress Disorder (PTSD), and traumatized early relationships may override genetic, constitutional, social, or psychological resilience factors. This means that abuse and neglect have greater adverse effects on brain development than genetics and environmental trauma. Preemies, if deprived of touch, are a prime example of "relational trauma." I have found that my patients who were placed in incubators and deprived of touch as newborns suffer from anxiety, depression, sleep disorders, substance abuse issues, feelings of loneliness, and social isolation to a greater degree than those who were not incubated and touch deprived.

How high are the risks of these traumas? Premature infants are seven times more likely to be hospitalized for bipolar disorder, three times more likely for depression, and two times more likely for psychosis than their full-term counterparts. These are staggering numbers. The damages can be mitigated through frequent body contact as a way to emotionally regulate and attune to the infant.

In varying measures, we all experience some form of disconnection. The degree to which we were disconnected from our primary caregiver is the degree to which we suffer. These wounds stay with us throughout our lives and affect our self-esteem, making us feel "less than" and unworthy. Unless...we heal.

Cindy and Roberta
Our Main Case Study

I want to introduce you to Cindy and Roberta, daughter and mother. We will be following them through the Nine Panel Mind Map journey so that you can see the progression *from* the problem of mother-infant disconnect, *through* the process of dismantling the problem, and *to* the paradigm shift into solution/connection. As you learn more about the Mind Map, you will learn about Cindy and Roberta's paradigm shift out of their considerable dilemma and begin to see how this same process can work for you.

"Roberta," late 40's, and her daughter "Cindy," early 20's and mother to 6-year-old daughter "Kate", came to see me in crisis. Cindy was on the verge of a nervous breakdown. Roberta was extremely concerned for both her daughter and her granddaughter. Cindy was deeply depressed, barely able to function.

When I first saw Cindy, I was troubled by how emotionally shut down she was. Cindy was barely able to talk, and I wondered whether we would be able to make a connection. Despite the fact that Cindy appeared nearly catatonic during our first few sessions, I perceived (based on her motivation to get better) that she was receptive to absorbing some therapeutic light. Cindy had tried the antidepressant Zoloft (Sertraline HCL), but it wasn't helping so she quit taking it.

PLEASE NOTE: Never get off medication—or any drug, legal or illegal—without the direct supervision of your doctor/psychiatrist.

Cindy expressed that she felt sad, frustrated, and hopeless. When I asked her to rate her level of depression and hopelessness, she rated both at a level of nine out of ten. I suggested that we increase her treatment to twice a week so that she could begin to express the repressed emotions behind her withdrawn state in a safe, therapeutic environment.

Roberta and I agreed that she would be involved in the therapy to help heal the mother-daughter disconnect. I explained that she would be instrumental in her daughter's healing, and that I would prepare and train her to help when the time was right. Cindy was informed that her mother was going to be an integral part of her healing, and that she had been quite curious about the process.

The cause behind Cindy's crippling depression was the focus of the treatment. Although she had suicidal thoughts, she had no plans or means of carrying out her wish to die and escape her emotional pain.

Her depression was a vicious manifestation of a much deeper problem. The real issue at hand was that Cindy had no "voice." From the time she was a little girl, Cindy's mother had made all of her decisions for her. Roberta smothered Cindy's self-expression and created a repressed, dependent child who developed into a repressed, dependent adult.

When I took an inventory of Cindy's first few years of life, I found the following Panel One wounds of disconnection:

1. Cindy was never breastfed.

2. Mother was not nurturing or attuned to her daughter. She was more interested in fulfilling her own needs than attending to Cindy's needs.

3. Mother was selfish and controlling.

4. Father was weak and selfish.

5. Cindy's parents fought a lot and were not strong, united, emotional parental pillars.

When Cindy came in to see me, her parents were in the process of divorcing. When the family agreed to move to California, Cindy's father chose to stay in their hometown rather than move with them. Although Cindy described her mother as a loving, stay-at-home mom who was kind and protective, she complained about her controlling and insensitive nature. Roberta micromanaged Cindy's life on a regular basis. Cindy was forced to attend dance class five to six times a week, starting at age 5. In spite of her daughter's apparent exhaustion and discontentment, Roberta pressured her to attend class anyway.

To adapt to the demands of her mother, Cindy became agreeable to everything at the cost of expressing her true authentic self. Cindy's authentic self began to erode daily, eventually causing a complete breakdown.

James F. Masterson, an internationally renowned American psychiatrist, argued that all personality disorders crucially involve the conflict between a person's two selves: the false self, which the very young child constructs to please the mother, and the true self. In Masterson's book, *Disorders of the Self: New Therapeutic Horizons: The Masterson Approach* (1996), he states, "It is not the rage or the hatred that is most destructive, but the sacrifices and compromises made around the conditions of relatedness that are most devastating to the self."

Roberta killed her daughter's budding sense of self by molding Cindy into her little dolly and unconsciously projecting her own, unfulfilled dreams onto her daughter. Cindy unconsciously complied with her mother's wishes in order to keep the mother-daughter bond intact and avoid "biting the hand that feeds her."

This type of toxic "hostage situation" of childhood is created when a parent uses the child to fulfill his or her own emotional needs. Roberta's unfulfilled childhood wishes, coupled with her unfulfilled marital needs, created the toxic mother-daughter dynamic that compromised Cindy's Big *I* (her healthy sense of self) and left her with a hole in the soul.

To Be Continued…

BREASTFEEDING FOR BODY, BRAIN, AND BONDING

In my Panel One inventory of Cindy's childhood wounds, I asked her if she was breastfed. Why is this question important? One of the greatest gifts that we can give our children for their health and future well-being is breastfeeding (more boob, less "boob tube").

Breast milk is rich in nutrients and antibodies to protect the newborn. As the milk matures, it has just the right amount of fat, sugar, water, and protein to promote healthy growth. Breast milk fights diseases like asthma, obesity, and Type 2 diabetes. Some research even shows that breast milk can reduce the risk of childhood leukemia and SIDS (Sudden

Infant Death Syndrome). Research also suggests that breastfed infants develop higher levels of intelligence.

But perhaps less talked about is the essential skin-to-skin contact that breastfeeding supplies to both infant and mother. Newborns feel more secure, warm, and comforted by this consistent contact, as does mother. The reassurance of continued physical presence to the newborn is crucial. It creates a sense of continuity from pre to post-birth life.

Gazing into mother's eyes, the baby comes to understand that he is loved, protected, and made to come first. Concurrently, mother receives hormones like oxytocin that promote the mothering instinct. This mutual bonding is paramount for healthy attachment and well-being.

I have seen mothers prop a pillow under their infant's chin and place the bottle in the infant's mouth (no eye contact, skin contact, or emotion), an illustration of how mothers are either not taught the importance of bonding (skin-to-skin, eye-to-eye) or simply lack the empathy to connect in this manner.

Now that you have discovered how the soul wound is inflicted, and how we as infants are defenseless and blameless for the cause, we will witness further, in Panel Two, how these early wounds translate into a profound reaction to the wound and a deeper sense of feeling "less than." We will further uncover the treacherous plot that has lurked unconsciously at the center of all of our deepest pain.

When wounds from our mother (our first experience of our inner world) and wounds from our father (our first experience of our outer world) simultaneously injure us, we become trapped in the double dungeon of darkness of hopelessness. The very caregivers who were meant to protect us and love us unconditionally made us feel unworthy of receiving (and later sharing) unconditional love.

Whether this was intentional or accidental is not of our concern at this juncture. Nature does not care why; it only concerns itself with what is. For the time being, we will disregard the reasons as well. Right now, we are sticking with the facts in order to uncover the truth.

Just before we proceed along the yellow-brick-road towards our own Emerald City (our desired destination, from *The Wizard of* Oz), I want to give you some concepts to ponder. In the 8th century, the *Tibetan Book of the Dead* described a form of yoga designed to make one become conscious while dreaming. In the practice of lucid dreaming, we become "awakened" to the fact that we are dreaming. Once we have this major realization, we are able to easily transform the physical laws that govern the dream state into any experience we wish. We can fly, shape shift, go anywhere, do anything, feel anything, think any thought, and instantly manifest our thoughts, desires, wishes, and whims into existence. In order to have this incredible, empowering experience, we must know that we are dreaming.

When I was five years old, I had a dream that I was in Cinderella's palace. Like most little girls, I loved being a princess. In my dream, I was running up and down a grand marble staircase, sliding down a wooden banister, playfully tipping over silver trays carried by waiters dressed in colorful balloon pants, satin vests, and pointy shoes. I kept shouting out, "It's just a dream! It's not true! I can do whatever I want to!"

As I began to shout out these words faster and faster, louder and louder, I began to feel a sense of power and freedom. The dream left a lifelong impression. It was the beginning of an awareness that I was the cause and creator of my dream, free to create "whatever I want to." The wisdom message imparted to me through this dream has had a profound influence on my perception of life.

WISDOM MESSAGE
We are the dreamers and creators of our dreams.
WE ARE THE CAUSE.

Ask yourself: What is possible when you realize that your misperceptions are simply nightmares that you can wake up from? Ask yourself: What is possible when you realize that you are the creator of your own reality?

Think of yourself as Dorothy, caught in the middle of an imaginary and illusory world, a world that was created by the masterful and deceiving Wizard in order to trap her into thinking that she is powerless to Be The Cause over the outcome of her life. Like Dorothy, think of yourself as trapped in an illusory world that was created by the impressions your parents left upon you.

Along your journey, you will discover how to dismantle your old blueprints and shift your consciousness to one of truth, self-love, and healing. Together we will shine the truth-light on your illusory past so you can eventually break free, heal, and Be The Cause of better outcomes for your life in real (versus Oz) time.

Let us continue to ease on down the yellow-brick-road…

THINK LIKE A SHRINK: CONNECTING THE DOTS

- Childhood is a hostage situation.
- You are not the cause of Part One of your life.
- Mother-infant disconnect and father-infant disconnect are the primary preventable cause of your childhood wounds.
- Your symptoms are clues that you were emotionally injured at *cause*.
- Expressing repressed, painful feelings in a therapeutic manner is your direct pathway to healing.
- Once you dismantle the old, wounded blueprint of your past, you can begin to *decode* your past, *recode* your future, and...

Be The Cause® of better outcomes for your life!

PANEL TWO

FROM THE PROBLEM: ENCODING

REACTION

"All parents damage their children. It cannot be helped. Youth, like pristine glass, absorbs the prints of its handlers. Some parents smudge, others crack, a few shatter childhoods completely into jagged little pieces, beyond repair."
~Mitch Albom

As you learned in the last Panel, when our basic physical and emotional needs are not met in a reasonable time frame, a state of physical and emotional imbalance is created within us. Without the capacity to self-soothe, we react to the wounds of these unmet needs with significant distress.

As babies, we are fragile and without boundaries, easily derailed emotionally, and prone to quickly breaking down into chaos. Defenseless, we are vulnerable to the darkness of psycho-viruses that eat away at the very core of our being. Entering us through the wounds of disconnect, these psychological viruses break down our sense of self, our health, and our general well-being, creating a vacant, yearning, hollow hole in the soul. This cavernous emptiness becomes easily reactivated later in life, leaving us vulnerable to being wounded over and over again.

Tragically, many professionals who aim to help the mother-infant disconnect too often are the ones that perpetrate it. Many forms of damaging misinformation comes from obstetricians, pediatricians, psychologists, and other professionals who retrigger the wound and generate even more damage and disconnect.

One popular approach to infant care was (and sadly still is) the Ferber Method. The premise of this technique is to allow babies to "cry it out" when discomforted in order to compel them to self-soothe. It is argued that this allows the infant to strengthen the ability to contain feelings and become emotionally independent of mother. This is utter misinformation!

Another equally hazardous practice is the disruption of the mother-infant bond far before its time. Unlike many other countries that offer up to a full year of maternity leave, the United States consistently forces mothers to leave their children with other care providers, usually after only three months. Experts have proven that this time frame isn't nearly sufficient enough to complete the development of a healthy human psyche, which according to attachment theory, takes over two years to mature.

Disrupting the mother-infant bond not only damages the infant, it hurts the mother as well. Many women who come to my office are filled with guilt, shame, and grief from leaving their babies with someone else. This break in bonding is often a repetition of a break the mother also experienced in her childhood. As she repeats the past with her own infant, it oftentimes retriggers her own childhood wounds. This repetition is so unconscious and subtle that her only awareness is that she does not feel quite "right" about what she's doing.

When will these so-called "experts" realize that it is the satisfying of the needs of the infant—not the deprivation of them—that creates emotional strength and the ability to self-soothe? Brain researchers, psychologists, and other mental health professionals now recognize that the Ferber Method and similar techniques that disrupt the mother-infant bond during the first critical two to three years are profoundly damaging to emotional and physical well-being. The "experts" are finally catching up to the perennial wisdom of attachment theory.

What does strengthen an infant's ability to contain feelings is healthy dependency during infancy. Through healthy dependency an infant can eventually separate and individuate without trauma. Through a gentle transitioning from dependence to independence, the emerging infant can mature emotionally, cognitively, and physically.

Neuroscience research attests to the fact that disconnection is not only stressful and discomfiting for infants but can also leave them less intelligent, less fit, more inflexible, more anxious, and more depressed. Disconnection weakens the core of the self and ultimately trickles down into the next generation, creating what psychiatrist Dr. Murray Bowen termed the **"multigenerational transmission process** of pathology." This is a fancy way of saying that we pass down our mental "un-health" to our children. Unless we learn to reconnect and heal now, we will perpetuate our psycho-viruses and infect the next generation.

At a conference on Attachment and Self-Regulation at my alma mater, UCLA, I had the honor of meeting Sir Richard Bowlby, son of John Bowlby, M.D., the originator of attachment theory. When discussing the importance of the mother-infant bond to early development, Sir

Richard said candidly and bluntly: "It's all about the primary caregiver. If we disrupt the relationship between the mother and child, we're screwed!" His straightforward words are now imbedded in my mind. Understanding the initial cause of our suffering is imperative to our present healing.

THIS IS NOT A BLAME GAME

The instinctive flow of nature cannot be disturbed without consequences. Attachment theory is not intended to shame, criticize, or attack mother (or father) for damaging their children. Parenting is an extremely difficult job, and most parents do the best that they can. Parenting based on the principles of attachment theory can lessen the damage to infants and children and/or help provide healing for the injured adult. The most important ingredient children need for healthy development, regardless of age or circumstance, is the parent or primary caregiver! This is the way it has always been, and the way it will always be. With the disintegration of the joint and extended family, parents have had the extra burden of raising children primarily by themselves. It takes a village to raise a child.

If all parents work together creatively and uncompromisingly to find the support and resources that will keep them closer to home and allow them better access to care of their children, especially during the most important first two developmental years of life, we can Be The Cause of a healthier next generation. There is simply no better way to lessen the damage to our children than to *be there*.

I can't even begin to describe to you the number of anguished children and adults that I see in my practice and the depth and intensity of their pain as a result of some form of parent-infant disconnect. The suffering of the individual and the family inevitably reverberates to our community and ultimately impacts the human race. Whether we like it or not, we are all interconnected.

ATTACHMENT AND THE DEVELOPING BRAIN

Margaret Mahler, Hungarian physician, author of *On Human Symbiosis and the Vicissitudes of Individuation: Infantile Psychosis* (1987), and creator of the separation-individuation theory of child development, speculates that after the first few weeks of infancy, the baby progresses from perceiving him or herself as one with its mother to slowly coming to distinguish itself from mother. Step by step, the baby discovers its own identity, will, and individuality. If there is a failure to separate and individuate in a healthy manner, or when the separation occurs too soon, the identity, or sense of the emerging self (*I*-dentity), is compromised.

Current research based on the developing brain of the infant confirms that the compromise is not only an emotional one, but a biophysical one as well. The reaction to the wound of the mother-infant disconnect creates biochemical and physical changes in the emerging infant brain that, if left unchecked, can create permanent damage in emotional and cognitive functioning.

The highly evolved brain involves the most dynamic processes in existence. The need to relate is a highly complex human function and is hardwired into our brain. The latest research on attachment theory and the developing brain illustrates the following:

- Our early relationships, starting from birth, create pathways that wire the brain and encode in our neural circuitry, creating blueprints for our future relationships.
- Negative early experiences shape perceptions and responses of the brain, preventing new information from getting integrated and interfering with our ability to learn, adapt, and grow from those experiences.
- Because the brain is malleable, new, healthy neural circuitry and networks, shaped by moment-to-moment experiences, create healthier and more resilient neural pathways.

Every experience causes neurons in our brain to fire. Repeated experiences cause neurons to fire repeatedly. According to Donald Hebb's book, *Neuropsychologist* (1949), neurons that "fire together, wire together," strengthening neural connections and creating neural pathways and networks that form patterns of response. All patterns of attachment are laid down in the brain in this way. It is also (thankfully) how these patterns can be altered.

The autonomic nervous system, the extension of our brain throughout our body, has a gas and brakes system of arousal (sympathetic) and resting state (parasympathetic). In order to keep us stabilized, this system needs constant regulation to maintain homeostasis, or balance, to continue to regulate the two aspects of this system.

When we perceive threat or danger, the amygdala, or primitive "emotional brain" (a set of neurons located deep in the brain that play a key role in processing emotions), prepares us for fight or flight. Under threat, our rational self becomes temporarily absent. Think of it as a sort of "emotional hijacking."

Research has proven "beyond irrefutability" that attachment patterns stabilize in our neural circuitry by 12-18 months of age. These patterns encode in our unconscious mind and disable us from being able to make conscious choices. Unless new experiences override them, they will remain the stable "rules" of relating, far into adulthood.

Researchers in the last five to ten years have also begun to understand more about oxytocin—the bonding hormone that is released through touch, warmth, and movement, such as with breastfeeding. Oxytocin helps to quell the fear response. This "love bond" hormone is why hugging makes us feel safe and bonded to the person who is helping to release it in the brain. Even a visual image of someone we love or feel safe with can release oxytocin in our brain and soothe our emotional dysregulation.

Healthy attachment creates a foundation of safety, protection, and emotional regulation in times of perceived threat or danger. It is based on a 3-part motivational system of fear, attachment, and exploration. Fear triggers attachment behaviors, and the safe haven of secure attachment soothes the fear of the amygdala, opening up exploration. The healthier the attachment, the safer the infant feels to investigate the surrounding world.

When parents act empathically to soothe the firing of the amygdala, the child can calm down and over time develop the ability to self-sooth. Without empathic parental attunement, the child will fail to develop the emotional bandwidth needed to cope with emotions and will struggle to develop a sense of identity, value, and self-acceptance.

The brain, the most complex organ in creation is very social. Scientists and researchers have discovered that the area right behind the eyes—the orbital prefrontal cortex—is quite specialized in functions having to do with attachment and interpersonal relating.

The prefrontal cortex—involved with emotion regulation, empathy, and facial recognition, to name just a few roles—is greatly influenced by the way parents attach to their infants. Brain research has shown that the function of the prefrontal cortex (PFC) is greatly increased as a result of secure attachment. The PFC regulates aspects of the emotional brain that have to do with body regulation, attunement communication, regulation of emotions, empathy, self-awareness, intuition, and morality.

Allan Schore, M.D., a leading researcher in the field of neuropsychology, explained that "the security of the attachment bond is the primary defense against psychopathology." What we can conclude about this information is that the pathway to a healthy mind and body is through connection and interconnection. We are not islands unto ourselves, not even peninsulas. Wired to connect, we are wired for relationships, and when we are disconnected *from*, we suffer immensely.

MITIGATING THE DAMAGES:
THE ROLE (AND SINS) OF THE FATHER

"I cannot think of any need in childhood as strong as the need for a father's protection."
~ Sigmund Freud

The father is often the infant's first experience of the world outside of mother. The father's loving and protecting interaction has a direct effect on the infant. If the father nurtures the mother, the mother can remain emotionally grounded in his strength, support, and resilience. The father's ability to nurture the nurturer has an indirect positive effect on the infant. However, if the father is physically unavailable or abusive, this direct and indirect negative effect will inevitably fail both the mother and the infant.

THE DOUBLE DUNGEON OF DARKNESS

The double dungeon of darkness represents the lack of emotional and physical nourishment from both mother and father. When mother and father fail to provide emotional and physical nourishment and support, the child has no place to turn but inward. Since a child is emotionally undeveloped with little to no sense of self, the child is trapped within this helpless, hopeless state and can easily deteriorate emotionally and psychologically from the inside out. With no one to turn to (including himself), the child is in the double dungeon of darkness.

It is the father's duty to help create a safe foundation for his child and aid in diminishing the damages of a deficient mother-infant bonding. Father does this by loving and supporting his partner and by providing the supplements of nourishment to his child that the mother is unable to adequately supply. In essence, it is the father who has to nurture the mother so that she can be more emotionally equipped to nurture the child. In cases where the mother fails the infant, it is the father who can unlock the imprisoning bars of the dungeon and release the child from feeling unsafe and insecure in his world with his mother. It is the father (or secondary caregiver) who has the power to mitigate the reactions to the wounds of mother-infant disconnect.

PANEL TWO: A VISUAL METAPHOR
FOR YOUR REACTION TO THE WOUND

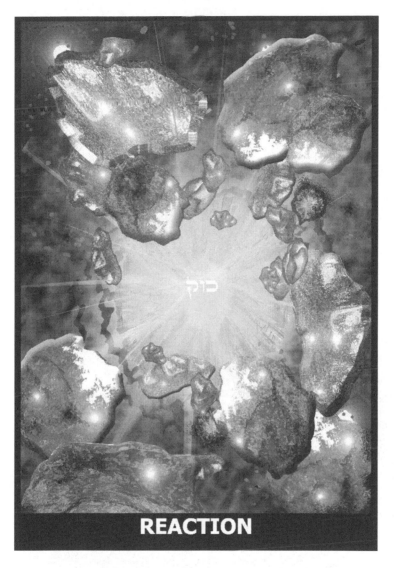

REACTION

Please study Panel Two. It represents the reaction to the wound of the mother-infant disconnect of Panel One. The white light separates into the prismatic colors of the rainbow creating a kaleidoscope of patterns and colors. This further separation into more duality represents the shattering of our wholeness, cracking our lens of perception and creating a perceptual distortion that interferes with our beliefs, thoughts, words, actions, feelings, habits, and values. The Big *I* is reduced to the Little *I*.

BIG *I*, LITTLE *I*

In order to fully understand how to shift our destiny from that of suffering and self-injury to one of healing and wholeness, we must first comprehend the enormous difference between the non-infiltrated self and the wounded, infiltrated self; I refer to them as the Big *I* and the Little *I*, respectively.

The Big *I* is the "tabula rasa" if you will: the perfect, unblemished, clean slate of our potential to be whole and complete. When we are given all the emotional ingredients necessary for healthy development, we can grow into the Big *I*, or the self- actualized person we are meant to be.

The Little *I*—our reduced, compromised sense of self—is the tragic result of the physical abuse, emotional abuse, neglect, or smothering that contaminates the clean slate of our potential and interferes with our ability to flourish. Fueled by the disconnections and conditional love of our parents, negative messages get ingrained into the very marrow of our self-perception and become our truth (we will see this in great detail in Panel Three).

OUR HIERARCHY OF NEEDS

As you can see, our Big *I* develops when our hierarchy of needs is met. Abraham Maslow, an American psychologist, introduced a theory of psychological health which shows that all human needs can be separated into a hierarchy of physical, emotional, mental, and spiritual needs. It is only when the basic lower needs are met that the higher needs can be fulfilled.

On a basic level, our physical needs for food, shelter, and clothing must be met to survive. When these needs are met, we can concern ourselves with our emotional needs: needs for social interaction and sense of belonging, to love and be loved, and for healthy self-esteem. When these needs are met, we can then concern ourselves with our mental or intellectual needs to learn and develop our reasoning minds. When all these needs are met, we can then focus on our spiritual needs: for harmony, beauty, order, unity, justice, goodness, compassion, desire to help others, and desire for self-transcendence. Maslow refers to people who have realized this highest state and fulfilled their own potential as "self-actualized." I refer to "self-actualization" as our Big *I*.

Although attempting to fulfill our needs is a lifelong process, what happens during our early development influences us the most deeply and shapes us the most profoundly. The deficits and injuries we experience as infants and toddlers will define the ways in which we see the world (and ourselves) as children and adolescents, and stay with us far into adulthood. These deficits compromise our sense of self and reduce our Big *I* down into the Little *I*. This "reduction" eventually shapes our core belief about ourselves (more about this in Panel Three).

THE POWER OF ILLUSION

To illustrate how difficult it can be to expose and alter a well-grafted illusion, I refer to Plato, the Greek philosopher. In Plato's dialogue, Allegory of the Cave, Socrates, his predecessor, poses a scenario whereby the things people took to be real were, in fact, an illusion.

In the parable, Socrates asks us to imagine a cave inhabited by prisoners who have been chained and immobilized all their lives. Their necks are permanently fixed, forcing them to gaze at a wall in front of them. The prisoners can see only shadows cast by men—not knowing that they are shadows—and hear only echoes of faint whispers.

Socrates suggests that the prisoners would take the shadows and echoes to be real, not merely the "reflections" of men. The prisoners believed the nature of the world as they saw it. Their entire existence depended on these shadows. Socrates offers freedom to one of the prisoners. Would the freed man recognize the shadows for what they were? Or would he cling to the illusion?

Like the cave in this allegory, you have been in a world where the lies have passed for truths, and the truths have been hiding in the darkness. Shackled and held hostage to your past, you, like the prisoners, are also trapped.

This is how the process works: you project an illusory, false self into the world, and the world reflects back to you. You then believe that this reflection is a representation of you when it is merely an illusion. I now refer back to the entrapment of the double dungeon of darkness: the darkness from within projects out into the world, reflecting back your (oftentimes distorted) view of yourself.

From your child-like perspective, the double dungeon of darkness creates a state of distorted despair. When both your mother and father fail to provide a safe inner and outer world and an accurate reflection of your true, authentic self, or Big *I*, it is impossible for you to "see clearly" and access your truth lens.

When the occluded eyes, or cracked lenses of perception, of your parents are your visual reference point on how you see yourself and the world around you, it distorts your own lens of perception as well. Just like the prisoners in the allegory of the cave, this psychoperceptual distortion creates a world where the lies pass for truths, and truths pass for lies.

Freud's repetition compulsion suggests that we get drawn back to this illusion and repeat these patterns until we lift the veil of the unconscious and see the truth. Letting in the light of the truth is the beginning of the process by which you set yourself free. You and I have already begun to crack open the dungeon. Shall we step outside?

Michelle
The Princess of the Double Dungeon

"Michelle," a 30-year-old woman of Hispanic culture came to see me because her boyfriend had assaulted her. At the time, she was using alcohol heavily. Michelle reported that she had been flirting with the idea of suicide for a long time, although she never had any plans or means of carrying out the act. Isolated from friends, Michelle spent many days in a messy house, bills piling up on her desk. There were days when she could barely crawl out of bed. She was in her own double dungeon of darkness.

Her choices in men were in line with what Freud called the "repetition compulsion." Her father, in and out of federal prison for the first six years of her life (he was in his own and very literal double dungeon as well), left her mother broke and in despair. Clearly, mom, the nurturer, was not being nourished by dad and had little to give to Michelle.

Living in an all-white and very racist neighborhood and then an all-black and very racist community, Michelle had very little, if any, family support to defend her against a threatening outside world breathing down her back on a daily basis. Neither parent was there to stand up for her when her brother and her peers bullied her.

Michelle came to treatment because she didn't want to go back to an abusive relationship. From a Freudian repetition compulsion perspective, Michelle was afraid that she would be trapped in her repetitive past. It is no surprise that with the parental blueprint she was handed, she had no concept of what a healthy relationship looks like. Like the prisoners of Plato's cave, it is impossible to see our shadows or blind spots when we live in our own double dungeon of darkness.

As an attempt to free herself from this psychological prison, Michelle immersed herself in self-help books, audio tapes, and retreats. At one point she reported to me that she had a huge wall of affirmations that she read out loud to herself every morning. Even with much effort, these self-help techniques didn't hold the key to unlocking her from her prison.

Unable to turn to her mother or father for help, she felt very alone, unimportant, and worthless in her double dungeon. Her view of herself and the world around her was a perfect reflection of her primary negative core belief about herself, a concept you will be learning much more about in Panel Three. You will be meeting up with Michelle again in the Panels to come and will learn more about how her negative core belief became entrenched into the fiber of her being.

Look at your life. What are the illusory beliefs that distort your view of yourself and the world around you? Shifting consciousness from illusion to truth is the key to your liberation of self and the pathway to your mental health. As your **cracked lens of perception** heals, you will begin to recognize that you are not the sum of your wounds, and that you are not the cause of Part One of your life.

The stories we tell ourselves, imprinted upon us long ago by our caregivers have been repeated over and over again. These redundant recordings become ingrained into our minds and memory. Lodged firmly in our psyche, these conditioned little tunes derail us each time when triggered by life's events.

These self-told stories of hopelessness and helplessness are our defaults and our fallbacks. These familiar fairy tales were stuffed into us a long time ago, and we gorged on them because we were starving for attention, love, touch, and contact of any kind, no matter how malnourishing and poisonous.

Then, we carried the torch for our parents and even protected them, making their falsehoods our truths. They no longer needed to fuel the fire of our self-worthlessness. We bore those blazes for them and are still doing so.

In spite of our awareness of their contribution to our mental un-health, many of us continue to idealize our parents and make their lies or misinformation our facts. They do not need to remind us of our self-worthlessness because they already "live" within our psyche as infiltrated viruses, encoded as negative core belief messages. The multigenerational psycho-viruses live on.

Cindy and Roberta Continued.

Cindy began to discover that her mother's loving yet controlling behavior and her father's sweet but selfish and unavailable behavior caused her to shut down and redirect her feelings of frustration and anger inward. The fact that the needs of her parents took precedence over her own began to significantly damage Cindy's sense of self-worth.

Cindy described her mother as wanting to make her into a doll—a plaything, or "mini-me"—in order to live out her own dreams through her daughter. Roberta revealed to me that her own childhood was replete with significant injuries of her own self-worth and self-acceptance, knowledge that would later serve both of them towards mutual healing.

As she developed, Cindy's weak father was unable to diminish his wife's damaging effects on their daughter and instead helped deadbolt the door of her psychological prison. Shackled to her aloneness, self-recrimination, and emptiness, Cindy was tightly sealed in her double dungeon of depression. You will learn more about Cindy in the coming Panels.

In *The Wizard of Oz*, Dorothy dreams about going "over the rainbow," a metaphor for her idealized reaction to being orphaned and abandoned by her mother and father. Idealistic, "over the rainbow" defense mechanisms serve to protect us from the excruciating pain of loss by taking us away from the harshness of reality. But the truth is, it is our fear and unwillingness to rip off the bandage in one shot that has caused us such ceaseless suffering.

The protracted tearing and shredding of years and years of avoidance, compliance, dread, and escape compounds the damage and spreads the infection. As we begin to acknowledge the multigenerational process of how our parents' wounds from the past interfered with their ability to parent, you will see how quickly and completely the house of cards will fall and set the stage for new possibilities for the second half of your life.

Before we move on to Panel Three, I want to remind you of Dr. M. Scott Peck's insight on pain and suffering and how everything that is happening and has happened to us happens for a reason. What if every wound, every cut, every abrasion, every lesion, loss, and hurt; every unwarranted slight, uncalled-for sabotage, and unprovoked injury was and is perfectly designed for our physical, psychological, emotional, and spiritual growth and expansion?

Whether or not you believe in God, a higher power, a force in the universe, a flow, or in nothing at all, seeing your pain, suffering, hardship, and darkness as your curse-by-design challenges will give you the strength and resilience you need to break free once and for all. This is your reward for embracing the struggle itself.

These curses are not just your crosses to bear but also your bridges to cross to a new land of possibility. Remember, without the challenge of the darkness, there is no growth. It is only through growth that you have the opportunity to shed your victim consciousness, give up the notion of being saved by mommy and daddy, and become your own hero.

THERE IS NO TURNING BACK NOW

You have made the decision to leave the supposed "comfort zone," the familiarity with the known, and the emotional atrophy of the status quo. You have consciously opted for the antidote over the venom, independence over codependence, progression over regression. You have chosen to risk it all (and what is it exactly that you would be endangering except the known suffering?).

This is not a painless process. There may be moments of anger, sorrow, and profound grief. There may be times that you feel like you are experiencing drug withdrawal. This can be scary, uncomfortable, and confusing. There may be moments when you feel lost in the dark forest. But much like exercise, which dares us, impels us, and drives us to push past the pain of our limitations, this journey is one of contraction and expansion, labor and rest, depletion and revitalization, and ultimately our healing.

The degree to which we stay conscious and awake to what blocks our light is the degree to which we can free ourselves from the past. The more we challenge the lies of the past with truth, integrity, and indignation, the better our chances to release ourselves from the tyranny of the miry dungeon and step into the glistening, prismatic sunlight of true insight, acute understanding, and enduring emancipation.

Now that we are aware that it was not us who were unworthy of unconditional love, but our parents' own wounds that made them incapable of giving that precious gift, you will see how quickly and completely the house of cards will fall in on itself.

Now that you have peered into the eyes of the truth and seen the great lie stripped bare, you will never be able to go back to the past delusions that have kept you in heavy shackles. The truth shall set you free; the process has already begun.

THINK LIKE A SHRINK: CONNECTING THE DOTS

- All parents damage their children to greater or lesser degrees.
- When we are disconnected *from*, we have a reaction *to*.
- Our Big *I* develops when our hierarchy of needs is met.
- Our Little *I* is our low self-esteem, our shadowed over, undeveloped sense of self.
- We carry the torch for our parents and make their falsehoods our facts.
- This process will not be painless, but ultimately, through learning the lessons of your "curse-by-design," you will learn to...

Be The Cause of better outcomes for your life!

PANEL THREE

FROM THE PROBLEM: ENCODING

ENCODING

"Genetic code is a divine writing."
~Toba Beta, Betelgeuse Incident

Welcome to Panel Three, the final phase of Creation. Structures created from the consciousness of truth, light, or health strengthen, grow, and remain sustainable in the face of stress over time. Conversely, structures created from the consciousness of darkness or un-health eventually break down and fall apart into entropy or chaos. Sustainability is the inspiration behind Panel Three.

As you grow and develop, the reactions to your wounds from childhood begin to formulate into thoughts and behaviors that begin to encode or blueprint into the fiber of your being. Think of this blueprint as your psychological DNA. We have seen how the mother-infant disconnect sets the stage for the foundation of our lives. We have seen how the father-mother/father-infant relationships can either become our saving grace or can entomb us inside of ourselves, locking us in the double dungeon of darkness. In this Panel, you will understand how the thoughts, behaviors, and feelings generated in our early infancy begin to take shape, forming the patterns that will develop and influence habits, attitudes, and lifestyle.

As these patterns repeat over time during our childhood, they reinforce our specific conduct, actions, and viewpoints. Inevitably, these complex arrangements of thoughts and behaviors groove ever deeper into our consciousness, forming a DNA blueprint for our destiny. You could say that this design draft becomes the window on how we experience the world and ourselves. This DNA blueprint becomes our core belief.

As spiritual leader Mahatma Gandhi said:

Your beliefs become your thoughts. Your thoughts become your words. Your words become your actions. Your actions become your habits. Your habits become your values. Your values become your destiny.

All get encoded into your destiny or outcome of your life.

When the structures within us are created from a "consciousness of light" (Source, truth, unconditional love, and good parenting), we strengthen, grow, and remain sustainable in the face of life's stressors, entering the world with a sense of safety, well-being, and value. If the composition of our blueprint is developed from a "consciousness of darkness" (criticism, judgment, misinterpretations, betrayal, abuse, abandonment, or narcissism), it eventually breaks us down, propelling us into entropy or chaos.

Take the case of Dorothy, orphaned and living in Kansas, barely able to get the attention or empathy of her busy Aunt Em and Uncle Henry. As we witness Dorothy's powerlessness and isolation at the threat of yet another profound loss in her life—being separated from her family by a tornado, another event beyond her control—we can only assume that her sense of value is further challenged. As she leaves the relative security (and misery) of the familiar, Dorothy is ill prepared for what lies ahead beyond the chaos of the tornado.

Her three companions are caught in their own negative core beliefs: the Scarecrow is caught in his own lack of clarity and self-awareness, believing that he has no brain; the Tin Man is immobilized by the beliefs that he lacks self-compassion and has no heart; the Lion is trapped by his lack of courage and faith in himself and regards himself as a coward.

Each character is suffering from a poor concept of self, ones built on falsehoods and fabrications. Each one's DNA is imprinted with these lies and therefore each character sees him or herself as flawed, projecting their negative core belief onto the world.

It is the information encoded into our DNA that determines our fate. Some codes are life-enhancing, others are not. The biological information contained in the DNA of a healthy embryo is the "life code" to create a healthy human being, whereas the "death code" of, let's say, a cancer cell is one of harm and destruction. Although certain aspects of our DNA are pre-selected by our genes (gender, eye color, height, etc.) there are many other facets that buck the absolutism of genetic determinism.

What I want you to take away from all this is that although your potential destiny is established by many forces outside of your control (heredity, conditioning, the attunement of your caregivers, socialization, and the physiological, psychological, and emotional outcomes brought about by experience), much of the DNA code that is passed down to us can be identified, altered, and re-conditioned towards better health and healing. Simply put, if you got a raw deal in life, you can renegotiate for a better one.

Doc Lew Childre, an American human development specialist and the founder of the Heart Math Institute, used epigenetics—the study of heritable changes in gene activity that are not caused by changes in the DNA sequence—to discover that the physical nature of DNA strands can change with heart-focused intention. In one particular experiment, DNA samples were measured to see what would happen to them under the condition of a physiological, mental, and emotional state of balance and harmony.

With heart-focused breathing and the emission of positive emotions of love and appreciation from Childre, two of the DNA samples startlingly unwound. The data concluded that "when individuals are in a heart-focused, loving state and in a more coherent mode of physiological functioning, they have a greater ability to alter the conformation of DNA."

Intentionality actually alters our blueprint. Isn't this amazing? This means that we have the power to transform what our DNA expresses. When we deliberately activate the coherent power of our heart with sincere feelings of appreciation, care, and love, we allow our heart's energy to work for us and refuel our reserves. We can actually nourish ourselves right down to the cellular level, offsetting the consequences that even decades of habitual negative thoughts and feelings have created. This is nothing short of a miracle!

At last you are aware of the awesome power you actually have to consciously alter how your wounds have impacted your thoughts, behaviors, and core beliefs. This is the glimmering beam of light at the end of a long, arduous tunnel and a beautiful way to describe how to harness the most powerful healing force in the universe: unconditional love.

BUT WHAT EXACTLY IS A CORE BELIEF?

Our core belief is the deep-seated, grafted-to-our-bones sense of ourselves, based on the totality of all of our experiences and knowledge from birth right up until this very moment in our lives. It is the meaning that we attach to ourselves.

It is how we see ourselves in relation to ourselves, to others, and to the world itself. Our core belief answers the blank that comes after "I am _____," or "I am not _____." Our primary negative core belief is based on false conclusions we drew about ourselves based on how our parents or caregivers treated us. For example, if our parents neglected us, we may believe that we are not important, that we are worthless or unloveable. If our parents called us stupid, we may believe that we are stupid. If our parents were critical, we may believe that we are not good enough.

American psychologist Albert Ellis speaks about irrational core beliefs. Founder of Rational Emotive Behavior Therapy in 1955, he identified what he referred to as limiting core beliefs. They are limiting because they set the bar in terms of how much you can grow and develop. In my practice I have encountered many negative core beliefs such as:

I am not good enough.

I am worthless.

I am unlovable.

I am not special.

I am stupid.

I am a mistake.

I am not safe.

I am a failure.

I have no voice.

I am incompetent.

Your negative core belief(s) is what you have been covertly carrying around with you all your life. Odds are, you've been trying desperately to hide your negative core belief from others and even from yourself. This modus operandi is a ticking time bomb that must be dismantled before it dismantles you. To prevent yourself from allowing it to dismantle and destroy you, you will learn to identify *it*, not identify *with it*.

PANEL THREE: A VISUAL METAPHOR
FOR YOUR ENCODING

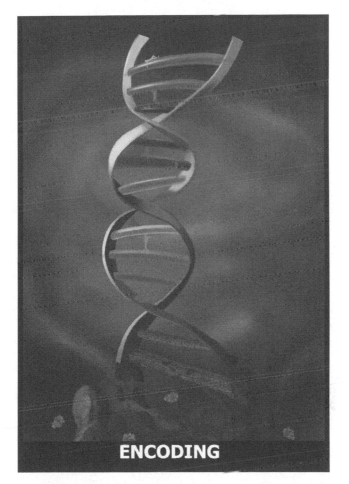

ENCODING

Please study Panel Three. The two strands of the DNA represent your pillars, or support system (usually mother/father), during infancy and childhood. Your pillars allow you to grow and develop into your Big *I*, or full potential. Without pillars, we lack a safe structure to support the development of a healthy core self and compromise our growth to the state of the Little *I*.

The little people on the rungs of the bonds ("lying around," "hanging around," "walking around") represent expressions of different types of your consciousness or intentions: your lazy consciousness on the one extreme and your motivated consciousness on the other. Notice the bonds that hold the DNA strand together. These bonds represent the information encoded, or the "code content," that makes up your core self.

If the code content is based on truth and integrity, it forms the basis for a healthy and sustainable human psyche. If the code content is based on lies and/or misinformation, we eventually break down into chaos (more about Chaos in Panel Four).

The spiraling ladder of the DNA strand represents both growth (evolution) and your spiral down into chaos (devolution). Like the game *Snakes and Ladders*, you're either climbing up and evolving or sliding and devolving down the ladder of life. The game of evolution and devolution is always dictated by your state of consciousness. As Max Plank reminds us, consciousness is *causal*.

Although it seems like our encoding is hard wired, we have choice points, moments in time where our destiny can go one way or the other. One path creates powerlessness and victimization caused by the unconscious psycho-viruses that downloaded themselves into your psyche. This path is riddled with painful relationships, destructive experiences and crises. Unconscious choices born out of our pathology, they are not really choices at all, but rather default choices, or allowances, if you will.

The other path is one of reclamation. It is the journey through the lies and negative core beliefs that have penetrated your sense of self for far too long. It is an excursion into the lifting of the veils of lies and the exposing of the truth. It is only through standing at choice points consciously that we can choose paths of growth.

You can unconsciously repeat the patterns that have saturated your life with suffering, self-judgment, and chaos. Or you can become conscious first and use this clear-sighted perspective to make healthier choices. and from this clear-sighted perspective, see the healthier choices in front of you before you choose.

Jake
The Smoker and the Death Code

"Jake," age 42, came to see me about quitting smoking. An avid tennis player and a pack-and-a-half a day smoker, Jake was sick and tired of wheezing and having to catch his breath all the time on the tennis court. He was worried that he might develop emphysema, a disease that recently took his father's life.

Initially a casual smoker, the habit and addiction took hold of Jake in college. Quickly, he was chemically and psychologically hooked. Jake knew that he had to let go of his addiction, but his smoking habit was a comfort zone. Although enslaved by it, he feared that quitting would cause him too much anxiety. Even though Jake knew the dangers of this death code, he cancelled his appointment with me at the last minute.

It is difficult to remove the comfort of a habit, particularly one laced with addiction. Encoding new information requires breaking of old bonds and releasing the psychological and chemical toxins held within. Jake's fear of quitting smoking won out over his fear of its consequences.

Examining your own coding is a process of observing, self-reflecting, and then deciphering and self-correcting the thoughts, beliefs, and actions that no longer serve you. The process demands rigorous self-honesty, integrity, and authenticity. Without dismantling your old bonds, your victim consciousness will dismantle you.

As with any structure in nature, a stable core survives and thrives while an unstable core weakens and eventually crumbles. It takes patience, honesty, humility, courage, egoless self-examination, and self-love to disassemble these faulty structures and rebuild a sustainable, stable, and flourishing base.

Fritjof Capra—Ph.D., physicist, systems theorist, and director of the Center for Ecoliteracy in Berkeley, California—devoted much of his work to the concept of sustainability. Learning valuable lessons from nature's ecosystems, Capra speaks of maintaining systems that can satisfy our needs and aspirations without diminishing the ability to sustain life:

> *The central challenge of our time is to create and maintain sustainable communities, i.e. social, cultural, and physical environments in which we can satisfy our needs and aspirations without diminishing the chances of future generations.*

Your central challenge is to encode your DNA with thoughts, behaviors, and beliefs that are sustainable. In doing so, you enhance the well-being of yourself, those around you, and the future generation.

As you know, thoughts, behaviors, and beliefs emanating from your dark, unhealthy consciousness (Little *I*) are not sustainable. They will eventually break you down. Those emanating from your light consciousness (Big *I*) lead to higher order thoughts and behaviors that are not only sustainable and growth producing to self and others but also contain the codes that break the chain of the multigenerational transmission process, freeing the next generation from human pain and suffering.

The importance of reinforcing your healthy codes or bonds, and dismantling your unhealthy ones, extends beyond the self, into both the immediate and global community, and on to the next generation. By constantly examining the consciousness behind your thoughts, behaviors, and core beliefs (the code content of your psychological DNA), you can begin to decipher which are most likely sustainable.

Sustainability creates the necessary balance and backbone to foster your growth and the growth of the human race. As you learn to distinguish between bonds that sustain you and those that break you down, which ones to nurture and which ones to destroy, you will enhance your ability to control the outcomes of your life. As you learn to honor higher forms of ethics where truth takes precedence over your rationalizations and resistance, you will create pathways to liberating your spirit and emancipating your life.

Please study Panel Three again. Think of the DNA strands and the bonds as the backbone of your overall health. Each rung represents a different facet of your life: physical health, mental health, emotional health, sexual health, spiritual health, financial health, family life, social life, career, education, leisure, etc. As you reprogram your life and integrate rest, relaxation, nutrition, therapy, exercise, meaningful relationships, fun, creativity, spirituality, freedom, optimism, and love, you become proactive in creating sustainable bonds that support the fiber of your being.

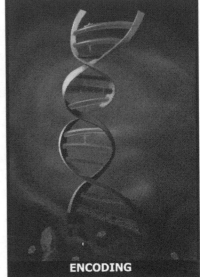

ENCODING

Although not all of us are fortunate enough to have strong pillars, or a strong family foundation, we have the freedom to intentionally choose new people and new encoding into our lives. Seeking health and balance through recoding your life opens up endless possibilities.

As I have reiterated many times, it is our parents' abilities to translate their emotional maturity, intimacy skills, and emotional availability that form the basis of our well-being. It is the messages from our multigenerational past that transfer to us and encode into our psyche. Let us put all the pieces together and see clearly how parenting styles of both our mothers and fathers leave their indelible imprint on our very essence.

PARENTING STYLES AND OUTCOMES

According to psychiatrist and father of attachment theory, John Bowlby, there are four attachment styles that babies develop with their caregivers:

1. Secure Attachment

2. Dismissive-Avoidant Attachment

3. Anxious-Ambivalent Attachment

4. Disorganized Attachment

1. Secure Attachment

If the parent/parents are responsive, available, present, predictable, and sensitive, chances are that the baby/child will feel safe, soothed, and protected. When the baby/child is attuned to, empathized with, and mirrored (their inner reality is reflected back to them and they feel connected with), the baby/child eventually learns how to self-soothe.

If the mirroring process between the baby/child and parent/parents consists of a mutual communication in tones, gestures, words, and facial expressions, the parent/parents are able to calm distress and amplify joy. Over time, the baby/child develops trust and a sense of safety, internalizing mother or caregiver as a source of comfort, and learns to seek connection.

Outcome of secure attachment: When caregivers are able to provide this type of crucial emotional nourishment, the baby/child develops trust in its own capacities to activate a response in others and learns that others will be there to foster its autonomy.

German-born, American psychoanalyst Erick Erickson, expert in developmental psychology, outlined stages of development we pass through over the course of a lifetime. The first stage of development, a stage he called "trust versus mistrust," is laid down from birth through 18 months of age. When our caregivers provide reliability, care, and affection, we learn to have a basic trust in our environment. If our caregivers fail us, our psychoperceptual lens cracks and we are at risk of seeing the world through a distorted, paranoid one.

With attuned caregiving and support for autonomy, the baby/infant has the basics to pass Erickson's next stage of development: "autonomy versus shame and doubt" (18 months to three years of age). During this stage, the toddler falls in love with the word "no" and realizes that he is a separate person with his own desires and abilities.

If the passage through the stage goes well, the toddler can separate and individuate and gain strength and independence. If the passage doesn't go well, the toddler is at risk of developing a clingy, dependent attachment.

2. Dismissive-Avoidant Attachment

On the flip side, if the parent/parents are dismissive, indifferent, distant, neglectful, or insensitive, chances are the baby/child will feel unsafe, uncared for, and unprotected. When the attention on the baby/child is lacking, the emotions of the baby/child will not be effectively regulated, causing him or her to feel rejected, withdrawn, and indifferent to the parent/parents. Eventually, the baby/child will stop seeking or expecting comfort or soothing, instead "numbing out" to anything outside of him or herself.

Outcome of dismissive-avoidant attachment: Dismissive-avoidant children are highly likely to become dismissive-avoidant adults. They inevitably become emotionally shut down because they are uncomfortable with intimacy, vulnerability, and dependency. To defend against the pain of attachment and developing feelings, they may devalue relationships. Not very trusting, they may exhibit hostility and aggression.

3. Anxious-Ambivalent Attachment

When the attention on the baby/child is pre-occupied, inconsistent, and unpredictable, the child feels insecure about the reliability of the parent for safety and protection. Not easily soothed, this baby/child internalizes the anxious mom, becoming focused on others and not on self. When a parent(s) is ambivalent—sometimes erratic, sometimes attentive and loving, sometimes harsh or punitive—the baby/child also becomes easily changeable, fluctuating between being clingy and possessive and being angry and defiant.

Outcome of anxious-ambivalent attachment: anxious-ambivalent children are likely to become anxious-ambivalent adults, vulnerable to abandonment fears, chronic vigilance about attachment/separation, and considerable anxiety. These adults may lack coping skills, subsequently becoming passive and feeling victimized by life.

4. Disorganized Attachment

If the parent/parents are disorganized, fragmented, dissociated, frightening, bizarre, abusive, or traumatizing, then the baby/child becomes helpless, paralyzed, chaotic, fragmented, or dissociated itself. That child cannot soothe or focus.

Outcome of disorganized attachment: disorganized attachment is likely to develop an unresolved/disorganized adult who has extreme difficulty functioning and regulating emotions. These adults tend to create dissociative defenses and are prone to severe mental illness.

As I stated earlier, parenting is the most difficult job in the world without question or comparison. It is the most challenging obligation of our lives. It requires an unswerving reliability, unfaltering emotional stability, and unwavering attunement that will test every aspect of our strength, will, resilience, courage, sense of self-value, and patience.

Very few are prepared, willing, committed, and emotionally healthy enough for the job. Be it by planning, accident, or any other variation, birth brings with it the utmost responsibility for every mother and father to rise to the occasion and attempt to raise—with every ounce of energy, good intention, wisdom, self-compassion, humor, and love—a healthy, happy, harmonious human being. Without hyperbole, the welfare of our entire human race is at stake.

When broken down from a nurture perspective, the formula becomes simple:

A + B = C.
Stable parenting + Stable infancy/childhood = Stable adulthood.

Securely attached babies/children inevitably become secure, autonomous adults who believe that relationships are generally safe and people are relatively helpful. These adults are comfortable with emotions, intimacy, and interdependency. They tolerate frustration well and are optimistic about relationships being lasting and satisfying.

TYPES OF INJURIOUS PARENTS

The "Auntie Em" Parent:

This type of parent doesn't allow their children to learn, fail, and persevere through their own trials. Adults who struggle with feeling out of control often micromanage their children's lives. The parent's sense of mistrust forces them to feel solely responsible for their child's success; thus, they hover. Sometimes known as "helicopter parents" or "smother-mothers/fathers," these parents create in their children the inability to persevere through adverse situations.

The "Scarecrow" Parent:

This type of parent doesn't provide their children the clear boundaries that build a sense of security and self-esteem. Adults with emotional insecurities often are more interested in being liked than being respected. This parent's immaturity compels them to worry about handling adult responsibilities. Focusing on their own needs more than on the child's, these parents act more like friends than parents, creating a mistrust and uncertainty within them that makes it difficult for their children to see the world as safe.

The "Great and Powerful Wizard" Parent:

This type of parent does not give their children enough face-to-face time, thus damaging their child's ability to bond. Adults who suffer from identity problems or feelings of inadequacy may find it difficult to feel up to the task of parenting. They may feel they are so inadequate that they pass on the responsibility to someone else who they feel is more qualified. Without stepping up and being the primary parent, these parents will generate an inability in their children to form lasting relationships in the world.

The "Over the Rainbow" Parent:

This type of parent has some unrealized dreams from their past that they try to fulfill vicariously through their children. Their children become their "little dolls," or "mini-mes." Unable to distinguish the boundaries between themselves and their children, they place undue pressure on them to carry out their ambitions. If the parent doesn't develop these boundaries by pursuing their own dreams through their own efforts, the children will come to resent the parent for projecting those desires onto them.

The "Endless Brick Road" Parent:

This type of parent never finishes what they start and fails to provide the tools their children need for success. These adults are generally not mature enough to role model a healthy lifestyle, cannot prepare children to meet their obligations, and cannot help them develop consistency and reliability.

The "Cowardly Lion" Parent:

This type of parent lacks the courage and conviction to lead their children and prepare them for life's difficult challenges. These adults are so in need of being liked and accepted by the child that they become subservient to the child's wishes. This lack of backbone produces strong-willed children whose personalities are sturdier than those of their parents. These children often learn to get their own way and go out into the world as bullies, unskilled at cooperation and collaboration and incapable of generating support.

The "Glinda the Good Witch" Parent:

This type of parent acts like a servant to their children, lavishing too much time and attention on them without providing real life skills. Sometimes referred to as a "smother-mother," these adults go to the opposite extreme in spoiling and idolizing their children. This reinforces a higher-than-healthy self-image in the development of the child that makes them self-centered, intolerant of criticism, and indifferent to serving others.

The "Elvira Gulch" Parent:

This type of parent is primarily concerned with obedience and perfection instead of growth and improvement. Adults who feel that their own reputation depends on their children's performance try to mold them with military precision. Their children may live in constant anxiety, frustration, or exhaustion just trying to meet expectations. These children go out into the world, believing that life is about command and control rather than love and empowerment.

Do any of these parental types sound familiar to you? Do you resonate with one set of poor role models over another or a combination? Are you seeing and realizing where our wounds come from and how profoundly they affect our lives?

LET'S DO A LITTLE PSYCHOLOGICAL DETECTIVE WORK

Although you may not remember the first years of your life, your childhood, coupled with the adult relationships you had with your parents, will give sufficient clues to understanding the cause behind your current pain and suffering.

If your parents demeaned you by calling you names, criticized you unfairly, wrongly accused you of lying, made you feel stupid, or as if your other siblings were more important; if they devalued you by ignoring you, treating you like a servant, or needlessly humiliating you; if they refused to spend time with you or showed you little love and affection; if they destroyed you by screaming at you, by betraying and abandoning you, or by smothering you; if they denied your feelings, abused you (physically or sexually), and punished you for speaking the truth, then it should come as no surprise that you suffer today!

Defenseless against your parents' messages—as they were defenseless against the messages of their own parents—you encoded them into the fiber of your being and repeated the multigenerational injuries. Can you now better understand and appreciate that you are not the cause of your pain and suffering as they, your parents, were not the cause of theirs?

Think about your own past and take a moment to comprehend the obstacles we all face when our lives start out behind the 8-ball.

LET'S TALK ABOUT NARCISSISTIC PARENTS

A narcissistic parent is a parent who was injured at *cause*. Because their own emotional needs were not met, they were not able to pass on enough emotional nutrients to their own children and fulfill their emotional health. The hallmark of the narcissistic parent is the Three D's: Demean, Devalue, and Destroy. This parent can be verbally abusive and/or physically abusive, emotionally and/or physically neglectful, or emotionally smothering.

Parents who are alcoholics, abuse other forms of substances, or abuse their children (physically, emotionally, or sexually), are easier to identify than parents who neglect, smother, or play victim to their children. It is the covertly damaging types of parent—those who instill the child with guilt, training the child to appease the "woe is me" denial of the parent's own failure—that often elude detection when looking at our earlier lives for answers.

A parent with a Narcissistic Personality Disorder poses a minefield of potential deathtraps for a child. The damage is more subtle but can wreak just as much havoc as the overt defacements. Although we have seen signs of narcissism in other parenting styles, a full-blown disorder is a torture chamber of pitfalls for a child.

Let's take a look at some critical symptoms that define a classically narcissistic parent. You may recognize some of these traits in one or both of your parents. A narcissistic parent demonstrates a grandiose sense of self-importance, often exhibited by an exaggeration of abilities and talents, or an expectation that he or she will be seen as superior to all others.

A classically narcissist parent is obsessed with him or herself, requires constant admiration and approval, is selfish and self-motivated, and gets furious if criticized. While there are varying degrees of this disorder, a narcissistic parent can be obsessed with power, intelligence, success, beauty, and love, believing that he or she is unique and special. Typically they hang out only with "special," high-status people.

Acting out of a sense of entitlement, a narcissistic parent can have unreasonable expectations, behave arrogantly, and may use their children to boost their own self esteem. Oftentimes obsessively close to the children, the narcissistic parent may use brainwashing tactics to keep their children dependent on them, even emotionally blackmailing them when they try to become independent.

A narcissistic parent may also enroll others to act as their "**flying monkeys**"—a term borrowed from *The Wizard of Oz*—and do their evil bidding for them. These "flying monkeys" may be siblings, other family members, or friends. They act as messengers or agents to further the parent's manipulative agenda. The victim of this abuse will oftentimes feel gaslighted, a term borrowed from *Gas Light* (1938), Patrick Hamilton's film about a woman who is being driven insane by her husband. **Gaslighting** describes a form of manipulation that seeks to sow seeds of doubt about perception and sanity, driving the person to question themselves and their experiences and slowly go insane.

Because this type of parent has little empathy and needs to be number one, this type of parent can destroy alliances among siblings and even treat one as a "golden child," using the other(s) as a scapegoat to benefit his or her own need for self-importance.

EFFECTS OF NARCISSISTIC ABUSE ON THE CHILD

When narcissism rears its dreadfully ugly head, the amount and intensity of suffering to the child is devastating and demoralizing. The constant tension to "keep the peace" and to not trigger the parent(s)' rage with "one wrong move" creates instability, anxiety, and a fear in the child of exhibiting thoughts, feelings, and rights. Sooner or later, the child is left feeling unimportant, invalidated, and inconsequential.

Parents do further sizable damage because most interactions come with strings attached. This teaches the child that love is conditional, that they "owe" something for the parent's benevolence, and that they exist only for the benefit of the parent.

LONG-TERM EFFECTS OF NARCISSISTIC ABUSE ON THE ADULT

I have seen the devastating consequences of narcissism time after time in my practice. It is heartbreaking. The adult loses out on a "normal" childhood (if there even is such a thing) by having to be more parent than child. They come to me feeling unloved, uncared for, and unimportant. Oftentimes, they feel like they are crazy because their mother or father has manipulated their sense of reality for so many years.

These scorned and torn individuals have low self-esteem, mistrust other adults, and are often self-critical to the point of mental and emotional flagellation. They are, more often than not, unable to have empathy or form meaningful relationships. They are insecure, codependent, and unable to make their own decisions. They may suffer from guilt, shame, and depression. They may also suffer from trying to constantly appease others (just like they did with their parents) and put other's needs before their own. Stripped of their true expression of their authentic self, they may develop a style of codependency that prevents them again from meeting their own needs.

Complex Post Traumatic Stress Disorder (Complex PTSD), also known as Disorders of Extreme Stress Not Otherwise Specified, is another outcome of long-term effects of narcissistic abuse. Traumatic experiences—such as childhood physical abuse, sexual abuse, or exposure to domestic violence—can cause it to develop. Complex PTSD is triggered by events that remind the person of the original wound. They manifest in the form of exaggerated responses to any activating event that may remind that individual of the original trauma. The reactions to triggers are over the top because the original trauma was never processed and resolved. These **WTF** (or **What The Freud!**) repetitive reactions cause others to think that the person is way out of line and/or crazy and unreasonable. These reactions cause massive problems in relationships, creating lots of chaos, defenses, and breakdowns.

The task of turning around their destructive negative core beliefs, unrealistic and distorted ideals, and seductive attraction towards abusive relationships with others is daunting to say the least. If they turn their defense mechanisms towards becoming narcissistic adults themselves, they will also treat others with mistrust and derision, like objects to be demeaned, devalued, and destroyed. If left untreated, their inherited traits and repeated patterns that started with the hurts of their parents will undoubtedly end up being passed on to their children.

Sometimes I feel that my job as a psychologist is to inoculate my patients with what I call "**anti-mommies** (or **anti-daddies**)" to protect them from becoming sick as a result of poor parenting. These anti-mommies and anti-daddies are delivered by educating my patients to protect their boundaries from emotionally unhealthy parental influences.

Cindy and Roberta Continued.

Cindy and I were now ready to discover her negative core belief. In order to discover a patient's primary negative core belief, I take a full inventory of their childhood wounds, their life, and medical history and begin to decipher the codes. What I have found to be the most effective way of uncovering the Achilles' heel core beliefs is to go face-to-face and declare them out loud to the patient, as if being said from mommy or daddy:

"You are ugly. You are stupid. You are incompetent. You are a burden. You are weak. You are not special. You are a loser. You are unworthy of love. You are a mistake. You should never have been born."

Inevitably, when I strike the nerve, I strike oil. The patient feels it in their solar plexus. Tears begin to well up, lips quiver, and the patient often breaks down crying. Out come the tissues (I call them "tissues for your issues"), and we hit pay dirt: the negative core belief is exposed in all its hideous glory. Once the repulsive, grotesque parasite has been unearthed, true healing can begin.

When patients (and you) have the realization that the *dis*-eased negative core belief has been spilling poison into them, contaminating their lives, everything shifts; the quiet understanding of what I have been telling them (and you) all along becomes crystal clear: You are not the cause of Part One of your life!

Cindy became curious about the idea of dismantling her core belief and confronting the deep wounds that catapulted her into a state of depression and ruined her life. The thought of releasing the poisons from her past was both scary and exciting to her.

After many conversations and connecting the dots between her past and her present symptoms, Cindy finally expressed through tears that she had always felt like she didn't matter. "I am not important enough to come first," she said.

The enormous courage of expressing her negative core belief brought her a sense of relief and a better understanding of how the wounds from Panel One had been devastating her mental health. Her emotional Achilles' heel had brought much pain and suffering, and putting it into words for the first time felt liberating. It wasn't long before Cindy noticed that her depression began to lift and her anger towards her mother—after being fully expressed—began to soften.

Cindy confessed that one of her biggest fears was that she wouldn't be able to be emotionally present for her 6-year-old daughter, Kate. I assured her that as she continued to "express her repress" (articulate her pain), her own healing would mend the collateral damage between her and her daughter, eventually leading to a more authentic and connected relationship between the two of them. Note that as the core belief is dismantled, the perceptual lie that we ingested, digested, and manifested in mental and physical un-health can now be unraveled, reprocessed, and rejected.

Cindy began showing even more symptom relief from her depression within a few weeks. As she began to heal, Cindy began to connect with her daughter more intimately and authentically.

Authenticity is the key to sustainability. Cindy's authentic desire to offer her daughter a brighter future by healing her own disconnects was a key motivating factor for her to risk the difficult challenges that therapy presented her with. Ultimately she understood that by taking the therapeutic journey, she would be instrumental in breaking the multigenerational transmission of psychopathology for the next generation.

MEDICATION AND SUSTAINABILITY

When Cindy and Roberta came in for their first session, they were considering a visit to the psychiatrist for antidepressant medication. Roberta was very concerned about her daughter's breakdown in mental health. Many of my patients ask me if there is a place for prescription medication in the Be The Cause Mind Map System. Some patients come to therapy on antianxiety or antidepressant medication and wonder what I think about their using of them. There is a time and place for these types of interventions.

Sometimes mental illness is due to organic causes such as brain tumors, injuries, or severe biochemical imbalances. It is wise to rule out these causes before jumping to psychological ones. I have found, however, that more often than not what we attribute to biochemical imbalances as cause can be traced to psychological injuries. If we remember that the mind and body are intricately interconnected and affect our brain chemistry, we can have a better understanding of how our thoughts create our unique psychopharmacology.

Here is an obvious way for you to understand how our thoughts direct the mind-body connection and affect our biochemistry: Imagine slicing a lemon in half and squeezing the juice under your tongue. Take the time to make this image real. You may notice an increase in the amount of saliva in your mouth, even though there was no lemon juice actually squeezed into it. This is the mind-body connection I am speaking about. Your body is able to biochemically respond to an image generated by your mind! Your emotional brain responds the same way. When you generate depressing thoughts, for example, your brain chemistry responds biochemically.

There are times when life's stressors can break us down and our defense mechanisms fail us. During these times symptom relief in the form of medication is a comforting option. Although medication can't fix the underlying cause, it can act as a temporary bandage to help stabilize symptoms while healing at the causal level takes effect. But remember, all medications have side effects (it's the cost of doing business with the pharmaceutical companies), so please consider this before ingesting them.

One way to regard medication is to see it as a biochemical cast. A cast can protect a broken arm while it heals, but once healed, you must still work to strengthen the arm to prevent it from re-injury and future breakage. Medication can shield you temporarily from emotional pain and suffering, but ultimately you must take charge of the underlying cause and strengthen your psyche or risk stunting your psychological growth.

Cindy and I made a deal that we would try treatment without medication first, and if she didn't get symptom relief in a relatively short period of time, she would opt for plan B and visit a psychiatrist.

While in graduate school, I recall being taught Kundalini yoga by a wonderful psychiatrist whose thinking at the time was way "out of the box" of conventional psychiatric interventions. He said that we can refer our patients for either medication or meditation. Today, more and more psychologists and medical professionals are integrating Eastern and Western healing practices that focus on healing through mind-body consciousness. I took his wisdom seriously and obtained a certification in yoga so that I can bring more mind-body-soul healing into my own practice.

I have found that as my patients heal, their anxiety and depression begin to lift, making medication less necessary. As you strengthen and grow psychospiritually, you may notice that you may become less symptomatic and have less need to go outside of yourself to balance your emotions.

Cindy never needed to go on meds. Upon her two year follow up, Cindy remains depression free and is thriving as a mother, daughter, and wife.

At the beginning of this Panel, we established that the original wound infiltrated into the fiber of our being, developing a DNA blueprint that got etched into our consciousness and formed our self-perception. We spoke about how Panel Three presents us with concrete evidence of how our thoughts, feelings, emotions, sense of value, and core beliefs get embedded into us.

As you begin to recognize that a negative system as it stands cannot be sustained, you may start to see that you are now on the edge of a metaphorical cliff, a crucial choice point that will decide your future. Your challenge is to resist the temptation to bury your head in the sand and repeat the continuous cycle of misery, embrace the truth, and use it to decode and dismantle your negative patterns to shift into health.

SELF REFLECTION AND SELF CORRECTION FOR SUSTAINABILITY

Examining your coding is a detailed process, requiring you to constantly self-reflect and self-correct. Self-reflection is the ability to consistently evaluate and decide whether your thoughts, actions, and beliefs serve you. Self-correction is correcting the ones that don't. Self-reflection and self-correction is a requirement for your growth, calling upon you to stay rigorously honest with yourself at all times. It requires that you stay authentic to your Big *I* and dismantle your inauthentic, Little

I based on illusory core beliefs. Self-reflection and self-correction are your main tools to embrace the truth and shift into health.

Just like any structure in nature, structures that lack integrity weaken and eventually crumble. When you live a life lacking integrity, authenticity, and ethics, you weaken your structural core. Lies, fear-based thinking, addictions, harsh words and deeds, judgment, lack of consideration for others, or any thoughts, actions, or beliefs rooted in victim or fear consciousness will eventually dismantle you if you don't dismantle them first.

When you live your life based on rigorous honesty, even in the face of harsh consequences; when you choose thoughts, actions, and beliefs that connect you to yourself and others, you create a sustainable and stable core self that fosters your growth and the growth of those around you.

It takes humility and an unconventional form of self-love and love of others to carry through with this type of egoless self-examination. It requires that you hold yourself to a higher form of ethics where truth takes precedence over defenses. You can't have mental health without ethics.

You have now completed the final process of the "Creation of the Problem" and have a better understanding of your choice point in the creation of your destiny and your opportunity to prevent yourself from falling victim to Chaos, Defenses, and Breakdowns. Take a sneak preview of Row Two of your Mind Map: Chaos, Defenses, and Breakdowns.

Row Two is a preview of the outcome of your "death code." Now take a sneak preview of Row Three: Paradigm Shift, Healing, and Unity. Row Three is a preview of the outcome of your "life code." Where you go next is up to you.

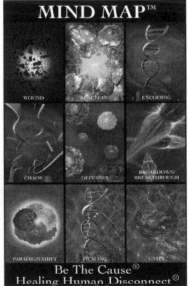

Most of us spend much of our lives in Row Two (Panels Four, Five, and Six), which you will learn more about in the coming chapters. Row Two is where your curse-by-design plays out. Going through Row Two can be a very destructive and painful journey if done unconsciously, or a very fruitful and growth-enhancing process when done with the right consciousness. Overcoming your curse-by-design can be transformational. Falling victim to it can be very destructive to you and those around you.

Much of the pain and drama of Row Two can be avoided by taking a proactive approach in Panel Three.

Either you can reactively allow the chaos of your unmanageable system to explode, hurtling you into endless darkness, or you can use your newfound knowledge proactively, to parachute yourself toward safety and healing. As you will soon see, the decision is solely yours.

OUTSIDE PERSPECTIVE AND SUSTAINABILITY

Sometimes we have blind spots that make it difficult for us to accurately self-reflect. We need the outside perspective of a psychologist, a group support system, or a wise and trusted advisor. A saying from Landmark Education about your blind spot comes to mind, "You can't know what you don't know."

One of the best examples of group support is the 12-Step Program. According to the Big Book of AA, rigorous and honest self-inventory is a necessary and important part of recovery. Those deeply entrenched in the defense mechanisms of their addiction view recovery as a threat to the bonds that hold their psyche together. The lies and illusions of the bonds of addiction are so strong that it is too risky for the addict to let go and risk the emotional chaos that they must face to free themselves from bondage (more about Chaos in Panel Four).

You may come upon times in your life where your blind spots render your ability to self-reflect useless, and a wise, objective perspective is needed (and oftentimes resisted). Part of healing requires that you submit to outside sources and allow their wisdom and objectivity to shed light on your darkness. It takes great humility to allow another to tell you truths that you may not want to hear. Becoming more sustainable includes being open to taking in other's wisdom and support.

HEALTH AND SUSTAINABILITY

The Be The Cause System also applies to your physical system and your health as key to your overall sustainability. No doubt, the mind and body are intricately connected. When your physical health is compromised, your body breaks down and becomes unsustainable and unreliable.

Look at Panel Three again and think of the DNA strand and the bonds that hold them together as a metaphor for the backbone of your health. Just as you are the cause of the outcome of your emotional well-being, you are also the cause of the outcome of your physical well-being. When

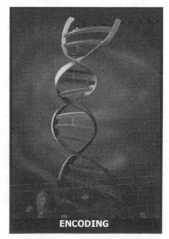

ENCODING

81

your physical health is compromised, it affects every aspect of your life, especially your emotions. When you are not physically well, it is hard to feel good.

Encoding your DNA with healthy choices means choosing foods as wisely as you choose your thoughts, behaviors, and core beliefs. It means choosing to exercise and build your strength, flexibility, and structural alignment for a sustainable body able to meet life's demands. When you encode your physical DNA with healthy choices, you become the cause of your ongoing health. When it comes to your health, ask yourself this: "Are my choices encoding my 'life code' or my 'death code'?"

SEX AND SUSTAINABILITY

Sex: The act of creation. According to Sigmund Freud, there are two basic instincts underlying all human motivation: the life instinct, or Eros, and the death instinct, or Thanatos. While our libido, or sexual desires, keeps us in constant motion, the ultimate goal of this motion is to be at peace, having no unmeet needs. Freud believed that every person has an unconscious wish to die in order to achieve this goal of peace. Perhaps what Freud was alluding to was another type of wish: the desire to transcend our physical being and tap into a higher form of consciousness.

Your sexual behavior, like all other behaviors, can be a manifestation of your life code or your death code. Through sexuality, you have the potential to be vulnerable, loving, and interconnected or selfish, aggressive, and disconnected. Through sexuality you can create love, interconnection, and life or disconnection, disease, and—even in some cases—death through the contraction of AIDS, a severe immunological disorder caused by the retrovirus HIV.

Your bonding and attachment to your primary caregiver, and how severely you were infiltrated in the first three years of life, is the blueprint of how you bond in your current relationships. Where else would your wounds be more powerfully triggered than in your most vulnerable human act? Sex.

Your sexual organs, the portal to creation, play a vital role in perpetuating your psychospiritual growth, enhancing intimacy with yourself and with others. It is in this act that love, passion, commitment, creation of life and connection to cosmic, or Source, energy occurs.

According to K. Ewers, in his article, *Tantra: The Path of Relationship and Creating the Sacred from the Mundane*, a synonym for "spiritual sex," or "sacred sexuality," is one way of liberating us from childhood wounds and elevating us to a higher state of meditative bliss—described by spiritual masters as the "cosmic orgasm," or the "at one" state of being. It is no coincidence that orgasm, referred to as the "Big O," is also referred to as an "Oh my God!" experience. It is also no coincidence that the vibrational rhythm of the sound of "Om" and that of an orgasm are mathematically similar.

When we connect sexually through mind-body-soul, we open the pathway to becoming "at one" with our partner. Through physical orgasm we can connect to the cosmic orgasm that connects us to Source and the source of the most healing force available to man: unconditional love.

When sex is devoid of the consciousness of unconditional love, it can become a fertile ground for unloving acts that can hurt us and break us down mentally, physically, and spiritually (another form of the "death code").

Casual sex, porn addiction, and make-up sex resulting from a cycle of domestic violence and rape are examples of ways in which we can use our sexuality to disconnect from self and others and block our connection to the source of unconditional love. As you continue your journey through the Mind Map, keep clear on how to align yourself with your "life code" consciousness and enhance your psychospiritual growth.

WOUND ACTIVATION PREVENTION SYSTEM

Life can and does frequently trigger painful reactions that open up our old wounds of childhood. The **Wound Activation Prevention System** is designed to help you process your raw amygdala, reactionary feelings, reduce the reactivity to life's triggers, and reboot you into seeing through a clear lens of perception so that you can regain your emotional equilibrium. Please use the Wound Activation Prevention System whenever life triggers you.

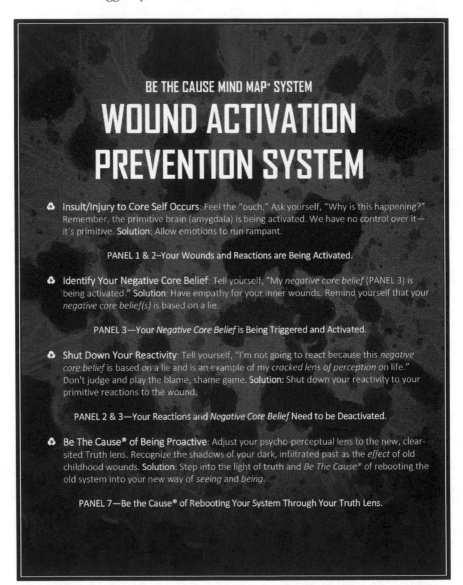

BE THE CAUSE MIND MAP® SYSTEM

WOUND ACTIVATION PREVENTION SYSTEM

♦ Insult/Injury to Core Self Occurs: Feel the "ouch." Ask yourself, "Why is this happening?" Remember, the primitive brain (amygdala) is being activated. We have no control over it— it's primitive. **Solution**: Allow emotions to run rampant.

PANEL 1 & 2–Your Wounds and Reactions are Being Activated.

♦ Identify Your Negative Core Belief: Tell yourself, "My *negative core belief* (PANEL 3) is being activated." **Solution**: Have empathy for your inner wounds. Remind yourself that your *negative core belief(s)* is based on a lie.

PANEL 3—Your *Negative Core Belief* is Being Triggered and Activated.

♦ Shut Down Your Reactivity: Tell yourself, "I'm not going to react because this *negative core belief* is based on a lie and is an example of my *cracked lens of perception* on life." Don't judge and play the blame, shame game. **Solution**: Shut down your reactivity to your primitive reactions to the wound.

PANEL 2 & 3—Your Reactions and *Negative Core Belief* Need to be Deactivated.

♦ Be The Cause® of Being Proactive: Adjust your psycho-perceptual lens to the new, clear-sited Truth lens. Recognize the shadows of your dark, infiltrated past as the *effect* of old childhood wounds. **Solution**: Step into the light of truth and *Be The Cause*® of rebooting the old system into your new way of *seeing* and *being*.

PANEL 7—Be the Cause® of Rebooting Your System Through Your Truth Lens.

THINK LIKE A SHRINK: CONNECTING THE DOTS

- Structures created from health strengthen and grow.
- Authenticity is key to sustainability.
- Our "negative core belief" is the deep-seated, grafted-to-our-bones belief about ourselves.
- Your negative core belief(s) creates a death code that, if not dismantled, interferes with your ability to...

Be The Cause® of better outcomes for your life!

THE PRECIPICE

"Well that's where we are. You say we're on the brink of destruction and you're right. But it's only on the brink that people find the will to change. Only at the precipice do we evolve. This is our moment. Don't take it from us, we are close to an answer."
~Professor Barnhardt

~*The Day The Earth Stood Still*, Edmund H. North, 1940

They say it's always darkest just before the dawn. As you discovered in Panel Three, not all bonds are sustainable. Negative bonds inhibit our growth and destroy our sense of well-being and need to be dismantled at once. Demolishing familiar structures, even misery-causing ones that have seemed to carry us this far in life, is inevitably met with defiance from within. I call this point of resistance the "Precipice."

As creatures of habit, we do not like change, even if that reconstruction promises inspiration, renewal, and happiness. As a result, we usually arrive at the precipice, not of our own accord but when the unsustainable bonds of our lives shatter and we hit our darkest hour.

Standing at the edge of the precipice and looking down into the abyss can evoke dread, terror, and total evasion. On the other hand, it can also elicit excitement, hope, and a sense of curiosity.

When a first time skydiver readies to launch out of the comfort of the aircraft into the unknown, there is a moment of pause where fear intermingles with the anticipation of what is to yet to come, and a cost-benefit analysis of the risk is calculated. The moment before the jump is a choice point: a golden opportunity to take a risk and experience something that most assuredly will challenge the skydiver's earthly limits, potentially morphing his or her fear into courage. On the other hand, it could also be a missed opportunity and a retreat to the comfort zone.

Just like the skydiver, we can choose to be proactive and decide to jump, or we can retreat, choose to do nothing, and passively wait to be pushed. When we choose to retreat, we find ourselves desperately trying to kick and scream our way back to the security of the familiar aircraft.

The choice to proactively take the leap of faith requires courage, trust, and support. The non-choice to reactively wait until shoved requires nothing of us. But once we have decided (or decided not to decide), there is no turning back.

We can plummet in free-fall, wishing desperately to return to the "safety" of Panel Three's accustomed, familiar hopelessness and bondage, or we can experience the fall for what it is—a moment where we as individuals are faced with a choice: free-fall without an attempt to pull the ripcord, despite it being firmly placed in our hands (where the outcome of this free-fall is quite literally in our own capable hands), or face the reality of the situation, become purveyor of our own destiny, and pull the cord, allowing a chance for survival. But this requires an acknowledgment of truth that many do not wish to face for one reason or another.

It should be noted that if you have already made the choice to take the leap into the unknown consequences of your fall, you do not then give up mid-fall and resign yourself to the same dejection that brought you to your precipice moment in the first place. The leap off the precipice represents your decision to jump into the truth, and once you do, it is best to just allow yourself to go with it.

AT THE PRECIPICE OF DRUG RECOVERY

I am reminded of a patient, "Jim," age 29, who thought he could be a recreational user of crystal meth. He found out in a devastating fashion that this was not possible. After an evening of using, Jim and his girlfriend smashed into a wall at 90 mph. Miraculously, they both survived. When Jim came to, he had a decision to make: either check into rehab immediately or quell the pain, shame, and regret with more of the drug. Jim was at the Precipice…

AT THE PRECIPICE OF DOMESTIC VIOLENCE

"Laura," age 32, was nursing a bruised eye as her boyfriend, "Rick," promised never to hit her again. He was crying, begging, and pleading with her that this time he was willing to go to therapy if only she didn't leave him.

When the police arrived, Laura's adrenaline was pumping. The officer asked her what had happened. Laura knew that if she told the officer that Rick hit her, Rick would be handcuffed, hauled off to jail, and Laura would risk losing the financial support for her and their 1-year-old son, "Miguel."

Would Laura have Rick incarcerated and protect herself and Miguel from his violence? Or would she defend Rick and cling to the only form of love that she knew? Laura was at the Precipice…

We come to the precipice many times in our lives. At first they are just quiet knocks on the door or subtle, little wake-up calls that attempt to gently shake us from our slumber. But if we keep ignoring the cautionary signs, they will repeat themselves over and over again in different guises, eventually growing louder and louder.

Inevitably, if we keep pushing the snooze button and ignoring the wake-up calls, they will kick the door in on us. By that time, we might be staring into the face of real crisis or possible death. It is then that we will have been pushed over the edge and forced to respond reactively to our critical circumstances.

In Panel Four, I will discuss the difference between proactively diving into the unknown versus reactively falling into the chaos. If and when your plane arrives at the perfect altitude for deployment, please remember that:

- You have already survived the original chaos that detonated long ago. Any current turmoil is a diluted version of the original. Revisiting it is your curse-by-design opportunity to correct what became shattered at the *causal* level.
- You are now better equipped to handle the next wave of discomfort. Your resources are truth, courage, understanding, logic, intelligence, compassion, and a desire for growth based on living life authentically.
- Your present negative core belief is already beginning to crack and dismantle. As you continue to self-reflect and self-correct, you can and will rebuild an empowering, accurate, positive core belief that will sustain you through the rest of your life.
- As you grow more sustainably, you will be in a better position to improve your life choices and create more positive outcomes in your life.

You are not alone. I am here, guiding you through the jump.

PANEL FOUR

THROUGH THE PROCESS: DECODING

CHAOS

"In chaos, there is fertility."
~Anaïs Nin

Chaos: A blessing and a vicious curse. The final breakdown of an unsustainable and faulty psychological blueprint that was created at cause, encoding as our primary negative core belief. This destructive blueprint must be dismantled in order to unlock us from our psychological prison—our double dungeon of darkness.

As a blessing, life's chaos can force us to break free from a lifestyle that would have destroyed us over time. The severely obese individual begins to exercise and change his eating habits. The depressed individual seeks therapy and proactively turns her life around. The compulsive gambler attends 12-Step meetings to gain control.

As a curse, chaos can wreak irreversible damage and cripple us for life. The alcoholic waits for liver disease, the sugar addict for diabetes, the smoker for emphysema or lung cancer, and only then do they attempt to turn back the hands of time. In all of these cases, chaos is the final breakdown of unsustainable bonds. But it doesn't have to be this way.

As you learned in the previous Panels, structures created from the consciousness of light and/or truth strengthen and remain sustainable in the face of stress, enduring over time, while structures created from the consciousness of darkness or lies eventually break down, falling apart into entropy or chaos. According to entropy theory, all matter ends in chaos. Nothing happens without making the universe more disorganized and disordered.

PANEL FOUR: A VISUAL METAPHOR
FOR THE CHAOS IN YOUR LIFE

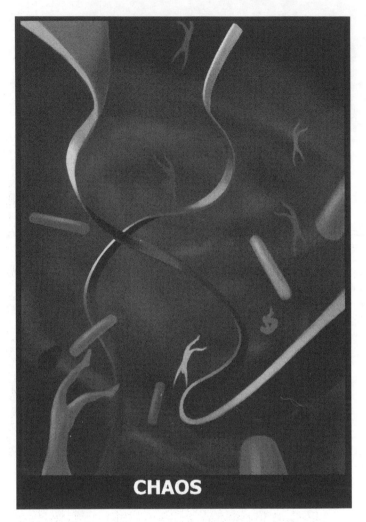

Please study Panel Four. Notice the DNA-like strands representing the disintegration of our core, the family unit and our core self, our parents/caregivers, our pillars, and the foundation of our core sense of self. Notice the little bodies hurling through space into the void of the unknown, signifying a state of confusion and disorientation that follows this disintegration.

The surrounding haze represents the release of dysfunctional thoughts, feelings, behaviors, and habits. The aftermath of this toxic fallout of noxious poisons represents the final breakdown of your defective core belief and all of its agonizing, confusing, and frightening manifestations and consequences. This dismantling, or dropping away, although seemingly threatening, foreign, and disorienting, actually serves as your greatest ally; it provides the opportunity to release yourself from the psychological prison of your past and recode and reconstruct yourself into a stronger, healthier, and more sustainable you.

As you begin to dismantle and *decode* the old, you will be more equipped to decipher the healthy from the unhealthy codes, and *recode* using principles based on truth as your guide. Ultimately, the work ahead is to shift your consciousness into one of self-value, self-compassion and self-love so that you can Be The Cause of healthier encoding and better outcomes for your life.

This process is not an easy one. Going from the false comfort of knowing into the unknown can be terrifying and fraught with danger. The uncertainty that you may experience from the feeling of letting go of your familiar world is merely your old wounded self, or Little *I*, trying frantically to cling to the status quo that kept you in a state of false security in the first place.

As you let go of your familiar world and comfort zone, the effects of the original wound will begin to reactivate so that you can—with focused, intentional work—choose to unravel the old encoding and recode anew.

REACTIVE VERSUS PROACTIVE CHAOS

"Reactive people are often affected by their physical environment. If the weather is good, they feel good. If it isn't, it affects their attitude and performance. Proactive people carry their own weather with them." ~Stephen Covey

Understanding the difference between reactively falling into chaos or proactively choosing to dismantle dysfunctional bonds that can harm you is the difference between being at the *"effect of"* or being the *"cause of"* the outcomes of your life. You are about to learn the difference.

When you are at the effect of chaos, you may find yourself feeling disoriented, frightened, and out of control. You may also find yourself feeling angry and resistant when bonds that were never going to sustain in the first place break down. Domestic violence, high conflict divorce, bottoming out on drugs or alcohol, and other such breakdowns in mental or physical health are extreme examples of reactively falling into chaos.

When you are at the cause of chaos and proactively dismantle your dysfunctional bonds, you may find yourself feeling liberated, powerful, and in control. Choosing to "let go" of destructive lifestyles and habits, and/or seeking help are examples of using chaos proactively. Being proactive means dismantling the dysfunctional bonds before they break you down.

Please study Panel Four again. The broken bonds of the DNA strand represent the breakdown of unsustainable and unhealthy thoughts, feelings, behaviors, patterns, or habits that over time encoded into the fiber of your being. The little people hurling off the DNA strand who were complacently sitting around, standing around, and lying around in Panel Three represent the dysfunctional aspects of yourself falling away from your patterned "comfort zone" of knowing and into the void of the unknown. This falling away represents a deconstruction of the old and eventually gives you an opportunity to restructure yourself into a stronger, healthier, more sustainable you.

CHAOS

The background haze surrounding the chaos represents the poisonous and toxic feelings released when dysfunctional bonds of old patterns and habits break. If not properly contained, the resultant toxic fallout can be hazardous to you, your significant others, and the community at large.

The dismantled DNA strand represents the necessary dismantling of the distorted self-perceptions that encoded into the fiber of your being at *cause*. These encodings—perceptual lies that interfered with your psychospiritual growth—must be decoded to allow you to continue to grow. The darkness surrounding the dismantled DNA strand represents the fear and hopelessness of being disconnected from.

Sometimes the damage from the disconnect is so profound that no person, place, or thing can help us find our way out of the trauma of the original wound. It is here in the darkness that many begin their search for a Higher Power. Sometimes the darkness of chaos inspires us to search for a pathway of healing that leads us back to the light.

As chaotic and destructive as this process can seem, this "falling into the darkness" can create new, authentic, and sustainable possibilities for new pathways to the light. These pathways are unique to the individual and may include artistic, creative, spiritual, and/or intellectual ways of finding higher levels of wisdom and truth.

Remember Jim, the meth user? He hit bottom by crashing his car into a brick wall and nearly losing his life. Jim took the opportunity and turned his chaos into his sobriety by checking into rehab, attending regular

12-Step meetings, and eventually entering therapy. As he began to identify the root cause of the disconnect that led to his feelings of worthlessness—an emotionally unavailable mother addicted to heroin made worse by a father who abandoned the family when he was two—he began to dismantle his negative core belief that he was unlovable.

Remember Laurie, the codependent love addict caught in a domestic violence relationship? She had the opportunity to hit bottom when she was punched in the eye by her boyfriend. Unlike Jim, Laurie didn't take the opportunity to shift out of her old way of being. Unwilling to take proactive steps to dismantle her dysfunctional relationship, Laurie refused to seek the needed support to become financially and emotionally independent of her abuser. Instead, she chose to protect him from the law and fell victim to repeated episodes of the cycle of domestic violence.

Initially Jim and Laurie hit bottom reactively: neither of them took proactive or preventative measures to deal with their respective addictions to crystal meth and co-dependent love. As a result, they all ended up at the *effect* of.

Laurie was unable to get proactive after hitting a new bottom; Jim, however, was. As a result of his proactivity, he turned his life toward the light and healing. Conversely, Laurie witnessed her life fall further into the darkness of domestic violence.

Proactively dismantling your death codes in the face of tough life decisions is not easy. Until they are dismantled and resolved, moving forward into the light of healing is virtually impossible. When you have the courage to enter the abyss of chaos proactively, you make it possible to move forward and become the cause of controlling the outcomes of your life. As I say in the logline of my novel and psychological thriller, *Lucid Darkness*, a fictional story about Healing Human Disconnect:

"Sometimes you have to enter the darkness to get to the light."

Claire and Hazel
Separation Anxiety and Mother-Infant Disconnect

"Claire," age 43, and her daughter "Hazel," age 13, came to see me because Hazel was suffering from separation anxiety. At the beginning of each school year, she would throw crying spells for days and desperately cling to her mother before finally going into the classroom.

During our first consultation, Claire and Hazel learned how early mother-infant disconnect is the basis for the cause of symptoms such as separation anxiety. As I took a history of Hazel's first three years of life, I informed them that we will track the disconnections together. Here are the disconnects we discovered:

When Hazel was four months old, Claire had to return to work full time. Hazel's grandmother, a kind and loving woman, took over Hazel's childcare, at which time the consistency of the mother-child bond broke. Remember that healthy emotional development requires consistent attachment to the primary caregiver.

The break in mother-infant consistency created the state of Hazel's *dis*-ease. Although her grandmother was kind and loving, full time care away from "mom" is too much time away from mom—children have no concept of time. Breaking the mother-infant connection created the foundation for her separation anxiety.

This scenario is not atypical in today's world. Fraught with good intentions, "grandma" could never be "mom." Nature is not as forgiving as we would like it to be when it comes to the need for consistent nurturing from the primary caregiver.

As I helped both Claire and Hazel connect the dots between the premature disconnection that occurred between them and the resulting school separation anxiety symptoms, they began to understand that the symptoms were merely triggers of the original mother-infant disconnect.

To help Hazel understand the emotional impact of disconnecting, I asked her to share with me an event that was of great significance to her. As she spoke, I looked down at my cell phone and turned my head away from her, pretending to be disinterested in what she had to say. I did this for no more than 20-30 seconds, but the impact was astounding! Hazel became visibly upset and anxious and lost focus and concentration. She didn't understand why I was "ignoring her."

I came out of my role-play and explained to her that I was giving her an experience of "disconnection." I explained that if my 20-30 seconds of looking away had such a negative impact on her, imagine what it was like for her at age 4 months to go without her mother's attention for most of the day (even though her grandmother was present). Remember attachment theory's emphasis on the importance of maintaining a consistent connection to the primary caregiver.

The "experiment" hit her like a ton of bricks, and she "got it." Although she had no words to express the hurt, anger, and sadness she must have felt during her infancy, she understood that disconnecting from her mother had serious emotional consequences. The injury occurred at a preverbal level, damaging her primitive "emotional brain" (the amygdala) and leaving her with unconscious, unresolved trauma.

In our next private session, I asked Hazel to express how it was for her to learn that her mother had to return to work when she was four months old. She said that knowing this made her feel "hurt, abandoned, angry, and unimportant." Although she could not really remember how she felt as an infant, she now knew that she did not feel good about her mother's decision to value work over her daughter.

During the next session, Hazel expressed her hurt about being left directly to her mother, whom I had prepared for the "truth conversation." As Hazel spoke, Claire listened empathically, neither defending nor excusing her decision to go back to work.

Knowing that she was safe to speak, Hazel felt courageous and comfortable enough to vent her pain to her mother and share her negative core belief: "I am unimportant and unlovable." It was this false core belief that cast a shadow over Hazel's emotional development, turning her into a clingy, dependent young lady.

Because Hazel was able to express the truth about how she felt about being disconnected *from*, she was able to begin to let go of her hurt. Because her mother was able to accept Hazel's feelings and reprocess the part she played in the cause of her daughter's symptoms, she became a key component of healing Hazel's separation anxiety.

Through listening and responding with empathy, Claire got to correct and heal the wound she inadvertently left her daughter with. Together, they were able to connect the dots between the past disconnection and her current symptoms. After expressing herself, Hazel said that she felt as though a ton of bricks was lifted off her chest.

Claire's ability to empathize with her daughter and listen to Hazel's expression of her emotional wounds permitted Hazel to release the hurt and begin the healing. Hazel's symptoms began to subside within a week.

It takes effort, compassion, faith, strength, courage, and love on the parts of both mother and daughter to enter into the "truth conversation." In the end, the greatest gift that Claire gave her daughter was to participate in this "truth conversation" and help heal the mother-daughter disconnect that Claire had unknowingly caused.

LETTING GO REACTIVELY

Sometimes mothers feel threatened by the "truth conversation," and the healing never happens. Rather than go through the process of confronting the past, some mothers choose to reactively let go, firing the therapist to avoid feeling blame, shame, judgment, or criticism. Please remember that the Be The Cause System's intention is to heal, not blame. Some mothers are so defensive that it is difficult for them to distinguish the difference between "I'm the cause" and "It's my fault," and they run before the distinction can be made.

Ironically, the same week that I met with Claire and Hazel, another mother and daughter sought counseling for separation anxiety as well.

"June" and her 11-year-old daughter, "Megan," came to therapy because every time Megan was dropped off at school, she would burst into tears.

June reported that Megan started daycare when she was three months old. During our first session I outlined three steps to healing mother-infant disconnect by applying the principles of the Be The Cause Mind Map:

1. *From*: Identify the problem of uncovering the history of the disconnection.

2. *Through*: Dismantle the problem by expressing the hurt of the disconnection to the mother/primary caregiver.

3. *To*: Paradigm Shift by reconnecting the disconnected relationship with mother/primary caregiver.

Both mother and daughter agreed to come back for another session the following week. Megan was eagerly looking forward to understanding more about her symptoms and how this therapeutic process could help her. Less than 24 hours after the first session, I received a phone call from Megan's mother, June. She was calling to cancel the appointment. She explained that she was switching to a different psychologist who would help her daughter with "coping skills" and perhaps medicate her anxiety.

Some parents find it easier to see the child as "the problem." Managing the symptoms or medicating them away seems like the better (and easier) alternative. Unfortunately, I have found that the symptoms only resurface and become more acute over time. The internal chaos cannot be contained for long.

DAMAGE CONTROL:
WHEN DAYCARE AND CHILDCARE ARE UNAVOIDABLE

There is no avoiding nature's design. Consistency and healthy attachment prevent children from developing a chaotic internal world filled with anxiety and depression. Returning to work too soon after the birth of the baby, placing the child into day care, giving over childcare to others, or leaving infants and young children alone for too long can traumatize the child and become the catalyst for symptom development. Nature doesn't care *why*.

The reality is that many parents return to work soon after the birth of their child, either by necessity or desire or because they do not understand attachment theory and the effects of mother-infant disconnect on the human psyche. To mitigate the damages, it is best to create as much consistency as possible for the infant/child.

Childcare provided by mature and loving family members (like grandparents) is a less damaging choice. A loving live-in nanny is a better alternative to rotating childcare providers. Whatever choices are made, consistency and unconditional love in the form of attuning to your child's needs is key.

Dr. Anne Green, a psychologist from Toronto, Canada used a very brilliant and innovative technique she created to help children heal from separation anxiety due to early attachment breaks. When dropped off to school, many children become visibly anxious and withdrawn.

To try to reverse the damage, Dr. Green created a game she called "Push Mommy Out the Door." When it is time for a parent to say goodbye to the child, she suggests saying, "OK, I have to go honey, so give me a little push, so I can go now." The technique typically works instantly. The crying and anxiety subsides when the child "pushes mommy out the door."

When children feel in control of the parent leaving, they don't feel the sting of being left; they get to be the abandoner—not the abandoned. The daycare providers caught on and took turns saying, "It's time for mommy to go, so let's push mommy out the door!"

Ariel
Letting Go and" Letting God"

"Ariel," age 25, came to see me because of her anger issues. She had a very dark and abusive past. Her father beat her regularly and locked her up in a cold, dark attic for hours while her mother watched and did nothing to stop him. When she was raped as a teenager, Ariel tried to turn to her mother, sisters, and cousins for help. Ignoring her cries, they acted "as if" they couldn't help or, worse, refused to believe her "story." When everyone abandoned her, she humbly turned to God to find the light in the darkness of her chaos. Life's suffering may not be this extreme for everyone, and not everyone believes in connecting to Source (or God) to heal. Ultimately, it is up to each one of us to find our own truth. Your pathway to healing is exactly that—your own.

Ariel turned to God during her darkest moments and eventually found the strength to form healthy, constructive, and loving relationships outside of her family. Through continued therapy she learned to heal from the multigenerational abuse her family of origin inflicted and passed on to her. Study Panel Four again and notice that the broken bonds have nothing to hold onto. It is often during times when we have nothing to hold onto that we finally "let go."

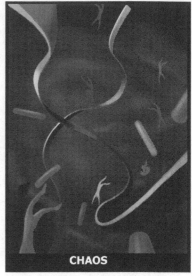

CHAOS

When we proactively enter Chaos, we can strengthen and grow, emerging victorious over our curse-by-design lessons. We have an opportunity to encode the wisdom into our new way of being. When we reactively and unconsciously "fall into" Chaos, we can miss the lessons, become victims, and fall prey to repeating the past.

Sometimes we have to fall deeper into the void to hit a new bottom and have another opportunity to master the lesson. Sometimes we block the lesson and defend against it. You will learn more about this topic in the next Panel on defense mechanisms.

Cindy and Roberta Continued.

At last visit, Cindy's anger towards her mother, Roberta, was lessening, and she was starting to form a better relationship with her 6-year-old daughter, Kate. Cindy's depression was also beginning to ease. But the old negative core beliefs, having furrowed so deeply for so long, are not so willing to give up ground. The resounding amplifier in Cindy's head—which for so many years echoed, "I am not important enough to come first"—doesn't easily consent to lowering its volume. We still needed to continue chipping away at her core belief with the sharpest axe: truth.

Now that Cindy recognized her wounds (Panel One), her reactions to them (Panel Two), and the formation of her primary negative core belief (Panel Three), it was time for her to explore and dismantle her Chaos (Panel Four), using truth as her instrument of deconstruction.

Cindy disclosed that she had no real relationships with people. She realized that she was disconnected from all those around her, including, to some degree, "Brendan," her husband, biggest ally, and childhood sweetheart. Even with Brendan, Cindy felt only just so close. Cindy began to understand that she had unknowingly built a wall around herself, making it difficult for her to make friends. The following truths began to emerge:

- Cindy didn't know how to plan anything because her mother had always planned for her.

- Cindy didn't feel a true sense of empathy so she was not fully present to people. She painfully described feeling like "a body trapped inside a person riding on autopilot, with their mind fully asleep."

- Cindy had a low capacity for stress and became easily frustrated.

As she came face-to-face with her hole in the soul, Cindy acknowledged that she was in a deep ditch of depression and needed me to pull her out. This breakthrough was her first authentic recognition of her situation and a surrendering to a vulnerability that would allow her to establish a healthy, temporary dependency on me. This dependency would enable her to leave the stagnation of the double dungeon and allow her to grow and gain her own power and independence.

Think about your present state of being and the struggles that are shaping your day-to-day existence. By observing your mind and your state of consciousness, you can get a better idea and understanding of the chaos in your own life, recognizing that, if we don't act proactively, we may need to fall deeper into the void and hit a new bottom before we can master the lesson.

As you will see in Panel Five, there are many kinds of defense mechanisms—some healthy, others not. Some serve us at particular times and through specific stages of our lives. Others linger on, way after they no longer serve us.

In the next Panel, you will learn how healthy defense mechanisms can be strengthened and made more flexible over time and how unhealthy ones become ineffective, obsolete, or downright harmful to us. As you continue your journey through the Mind Map, remember that breakdowns are new opportunities to break *through*.

"In the space between chaos and shape, there was another chance."
~ Jeanette Winterson, *The World and Other Places*

THINK LIKE A SHRINK: CONNECTING THE DOTS

- Human Disconnect results in emotional chaos.
- Bonds that are unsustainable will break down.
- You can choose to let go proactively before you are forced to let go reactively.
- Chaos is both a blessing and a curse—by design.
- Dismantling old unsustainable codes gives you the opportunity to recode into health.
- Letting go is key to healing.
- Breaking old multigenerational patterns breaks you out of the double dungeon of darkness, allowing you to be free to…

Be The Cause® of better outcomes for your life!

PANEL FIVE

THROUGH THE PROCESS: DECODING

DEFENSES

"Symptoms Don't Lie—They Point to the Cause of Your Psychopathology."
~ Dr. Judy

Your symptoms don't lie. They are the hieroglyphics or clues that help you identify and guide you to the "root cause" of psychopathology—Human Disconnect. The anxiety and depression of being disconnected *from* naturally causes you to build adaptive defense mechanisms designed to shield you from these painful emotions. Although your defense mechanisms start off as adaptive solutions to your problems, they eventually become the problem when you continue to "defend" after the threat of disconnection is gone. Your defense mechanisms, when no longer functional, eventually become your symptoms.

As you learned in Panel One, most psychopathology begins with mother-infant disconnect, leaving you vulnerable to being infiltrated with misinformation that integrates into the fiber of your being and "miscodes" into a negative core belief. This miscoding creates a cracked psychoperceptual view of yourself and the world around you, affecting your self-esteem and eroding your ability to see yourself and others clearly.

To defend against painful feelings of low self-esteem, you develop defense mechanisms to protect yourself from your negative core beliefs about yourself. Alcohol abuse (or any other form of substance abuse), gambling, isolating, sex addiction, and overeating are all examples of defense mechanisms. Defense mechanisms temporarily alleviate the feelings that they are meant to protect—feelings of anxiety, depression, fear and other negative emotions that become triggered by life. The problem is that they eventually break down and—break you down—in the process.

Just like the Wizard created the illusory Land of Oz, your wounds from the past created your distorted and illusory world. To defend against your own painful Oz-like illusions, you created defense mechanisms that block you from seeing the truth of the illusion. Coming full circle, these defense mechanisms are your clues that injury happened at cause.

As a desperate attempt to communicate their unconscious message, your *isms* (defense mechanisms) will continue to grow, mentally and physically breaking you down or smothering you in the process. Until you wake up and pay attention to the cause behind them, isms must be there to continue to "speak" to you or "yell" at you. The more you ignore or deny the truth behind cause and the lessons contained within the isms, the louder and stronger the signals become. Your isms are your wake up call.

Your isms are personal to the type of injury inflicted on you and the particular way in which you cope. Although they intend to help, they end up creating more chaos in your life (think of a drug addict using the drug to numb the pain).

Addictions, obsessions, or psychosomatic symptoms manifesting in the body—such as tension headaches and backaches—are examples of ways symptoms function to distract you from dealing with the truth behind cause. These symptoms represent your suppressed and unresolved feelings. They interfere with the possibility of creating a healthy future.

Most people choose to keep the past where they think it belongs: in the past. Unfortunately, the more we bury the past, the more it haunts our present. Wounds from the past don't disappear because we deny their existence. On the contrary, unresolved wounds from Panel One manifest as the isms of Panel Five.

CONFRONTING THE CAUSE OF THE ORIGINAL WOUND

Our biggest fear—and the reason we are most defended as a human race—has everything to do with mother-infant disconnect, the original cause of all psychopathology. It is this painful disconnect that we keep defending against for the rest of our lives. Too threatening to deal with directly, the original wound gets pushed out of our conscious awareness, resurfacing later as our defense mechanisms. They can only remain in this form for so long before the anxiety and depression contained within the isms breaks through, reminding us that erecting defenses against the original cause isn't the real solution to the problem.

In a pattern that Dr. Sigmund Freud called the "repetition compulsion," the theme of the effects of the wound of the disconnect repeat within ourselves, between our relationships, and even globally. The theme continues to play out in the "here and now" in an attempt to wake us up and remind us to resolve our infiltrations on a causal level.

The global, macro picture of the effects of mother-infant disconnect is a mirror and hologram of Human Disconnect "gone viral." The effects of Global Disconnect are an even more ominous and acute reason to resolve the problem of Human Disconnect at *cause*.

Global Disconnect—the pathway to the annihilation of the human race—occurs when our collective infiltrations (Little I's) mass-project out into our world, creating a global double dungeon effect. Collectively unsafe on the inside, we project and create a state of global danger in the world around us. We can see our disconnected and fragmented selves mirrored back to us in the form of a disconnected and fragmented humanity.

War, mass suicides, and homicides (including rampant public shootings) are examples of symptoms of a fractured human race "gone symptomatic" on a macro scale. We can look at the symptoms and wonder why, but until we tell the truth of what causes people to break down into chaos and destroy others and themselves, we will be stuck in denial or in symptom management mode (at best).

Therapies including medication, cognitive and/or behavior management, positive affirmations, or any type of symptom management technique, are some of our best attempts at putting a temporary bandage on the mother-infant disconnect. These management techniques are not only failing to cure us but also, more significantly, enabling us to continuously to deny the truth.

Until we understand that psychopathology begins with mother-child "bonding-gone-wrong," until we deal with the prevention and healing of Human Disconnect at the causal level, we cannot heal individually or globally. Most people don't want to tread on these "emotionally dangerous" grounds. Most people don't want to "go there" and deal with the original wound.

THE HIDDEN CAUSE

"Three things cannot be long hidden: the sun, the moon, and the truth." ~ Buddha

Because the original wound occurs at an early age and stage of development, prior to our ability to process the information logically, its cause remains hidden in our unconscious. Although we have no memory or words to describe what happened, we can see the evidence of the original injuries in our symptoms. Recall: symptoms don't lie. They are the "language" communicating to us what happened at cause. If preverbal and unconscious injuries are not made conscious, they manifest as our symptoms. There are reasons as to why the cause of the wound is hidden.

Tristan
Denial of the Original Wound

"Tristan," age 47, was the last of seven children. Her mother, overworked and overwhelmed, was one of the most giving women in the world. Because her mother was so exhausted from taking care of her many children and demanding husband, she had little time left to give to her youngest daughter.

When Tristan needed attention from her mother, she had to wait her turn. Her basic narcissistic supplies (core needs for healthy emotional development) were not met quickly enough. The need for consistent touch, eye contact, and regular feedings went unmet for too long. The frustration of waiting, coupled with her inability to self-soothe, created a state of emotional pain due to unmet needs. Tristan developed "anxious attachment."

Anxious-ambivalent, insecure attachment occurs when infants like Tristan are not attended to in a consistent and timely manner. The frustration of waiting creates a state of emotional pain due to unmet needs. These infants are inconsolable and don't calm down when mother returns. As adults, they can become overly dependent, doubting their worth in relationships and using relationships to define who they are.

This attachment style leads to jealousy, control, and clingy or domineering behavior. Tending to feel unappreciated in relationships, they worry that their partner doesn't love them or will leave them. After a fight they feel unloved, preparing for loss by threatening and sabotaging the relationship before they are left.

It is not until later in life that reactions to unmet needs turn into anger, frustration, poor relationship skills, and low self-esteem. These unconscious feelings remain suppressed until they re-emerge later in life in the form of well-developed defense mechanisms—strategic mechanisms designed to hide and suppress the cause.

Food as a Defense Mechanism

When Tristan came in to see me for her first session, she was distraught because she was 50 pounds overweight. The mere suggestion that her weight had to do with her mother's inability to meet her emotional needs was met with extreme resistance. The mention of mother-infant disconnect as an explanation for her weight gain caused her to block her ears in defense. Many times she threatened to leave the office, warning me not to "attack" her mother, whom she described as the most wonderful, loving mother in the whole world. Because she idealized her mother, Tristan ignored the fact that her mother, in spite of her best efforts, failed to provide for Tristan's basic emotional needs.

Remember, there are reasons why *cause* is hidden...

The brilliant psychoanalyst Alice Miller speaks of the threat of confronting mother for abandoning our childhood needs. Referring back to her classic book *Drama of the Gifted Child: The Search for the True Self*, she talks about how a child would rather be "a bad child in a good world than a good child in a bad world." Rather than live in a dangerous world where mother doesn't provide for our needs or, worse, doesn't care, we need to preserve her idealized image in order to emotionally survive. Rather than see our parents as the cause of our pain and suffering, it is safer to blame ourselves. To survive, we cannot bite the hand that feeds us.

Over the course of therapy, Tristan began to connect the dots between her neediness, her low self-esteem, and the possibility of the idea that perhaps her mother—too tired and occupied to attend to her—was unable to give enough. Though Tristan defended her mother's struggle to give more, she was limited in her availability. She finally understood that it was not a matter of blame but a matter of fact. Based on her childhood circumstances, she concluded (not surprisingly), "I'm not worth much."

As a part of the "repetition compulsion" theme of the wound, Tristan surrounded herself with friends who wouldn't pay enough attention to her and formed relationships with men who wouldn't make her important enough to commit to her. To exacerbate matters, she used food as a defense mechanism to soothe the pain of not feeling important. Her resultant weight gain further defended her against forming relationships that could hurt and disappoint her once again.

By overeating, she created her double dungeon. By masking her dark, unworthy feelings and low self-esteem through binging, she projected the darkness of being overweight out into the world. When she felt that the world was rejecting her for being overweight, she felt the need to defend herself even more. This unconscious cycle of self-sabotage validated her fear and suspicion that she was not worth much after all.

Though Tristan thought she was protecting herself, she was really protecting her mother against her unexpressed anger and hurt. By shoving her pain, anger, and frustration down with food, she medicated away her authentic feelings. Food is often used as a way of filling the hole in the soul and as a way to "connect" to mother's nourishment.

I often say to patients, "The more you protect your mother in your therapeutic process, the more symptomatic you stay." I also often say to my patients, "The more you defend your mother, the slower you heal."

Isolationism

Tristan's "emotional blackouts"—the silent treatment she inflicted on those who fell short in their ability to make her feel special—were her way of making others feel guilty for not giving her enough. Deflecting her unexpressed anger and hurt, she spared her mother the expression of her authentic feelings and instead punished her own friends by cutting them off when they didn't give "enough."

The frustration of waiting too long to get her needs met, coupled with her inability to self soothe, created a state of anxiety. When the anxiety became overwhelming, she retreated into isolationism. Isolationism is created when the infant receives little attention in the first few years of life.

Unlike anxious babies who live in a constant state of need, avoidant babies have given up on receiving love. Over time, they figure out that mother's need is to not be needed. To protect their protector, they "comply" by detaching. When Tristan thought that she was becoming too needy, she complied by detaching. Tristan fluctuated between exhibiting symptoms of "anxious attachment" and "avoidant attachment."

Infants who were detached *from* in early infancy grow up detached from others. They avoid intimacy by withdrawing into computers, television, and other isolationist activities. It is their way of protecting themselves from getting too emotionally close.

Isolating a person from other human beings is one of the cruelest forms of punishment known to man. The use of solitary confinement in prisons is known to drive people insane. Psychologist Terry Kupers says that solitary confinement "destroys people as human beings." Increases in anxiety, depression, anger, cognitive disturbances, paranoia, perceptual distortions, psychosis, and suicide attempts are some of the consequences of solitary confinement—more evidence for the damaging effects of Human Disconnect.

Tom
Sexual Dysfunction as a Defense Against Intimacy

"Tom," age 37, came into therapy because his wife complained that he was on the computer most evenings watching porn. Their infrequent sex life was devoid of eye contact, foreplay, and affection. "I feel like a blow up doll when I'm with him," she complained. She may as well have been. Tossed aside after he was sexually satisfied, she was left feeling emptier after the experience than before. Their sexual connection (or lack thereof) reinforced her core belief: "I'm not special."

It is no surprise that symptoms of Human Disconnect "attack" the organs of creation. The act of sexual intercourse—the highest form of pleasure available to man and a place where mind, body, and soul interconnect—can also be an act of disconnection. As Tom's wife expressed, sex with her husband left her feeling used and disconnected *from*. Tom, although sexually gratified in the moment of orgasm, felt empty and meaningless after the act as well.

Notice that one person's ism will attract and trigger another person's ism. If left unresolved, each individual will continue to trigger the other until there is a breakdown in the self and/or the relationship (more about that in Panel Six). Recall from Panel Three that dysfunctional habits—encoded as thoughts, feelings, and behaviors—break down into Chaos (Panel Four) and form the isms of Panel Five. Recall that isms are the full-blown manifestation of the wounds of Panel One. Isms serve the important function of keeping you from feeling the injuries of your Panel One wounds. They keep you in denial of the cause and protect you from seeing mother as less than good. They keep you from biting the hand that feeds you.

Tom's emotional injury of being avoided (avoidant attachment) attracted his wife's emotional injury of being ignored (anxious attachment), causing them to trigger each other's negative core beliefs. Their mutual unconscious and unresolved wounds created a repetition of these old patterns.

When I do couples therapy, I observe each person triggering the other person's negative core belief and how those core beliefs break down the relationship. As long as the couple remains unconscious to the cause of the breakdown, they will keep repeating and reinjuring each other. The "WTF" cycle continues until they stop projecting the pain onto each other and redirect it back to cause.

LABELISM

"As soon as you believe that a label you've put on yourself is true, you've limited something that is literally limitless, you've limited who you are into nothing but a thought."
~Adyashanti

A very subtle and popular ism rampant in our psychological and medical profession is a term I like to refer to as "labelism". Labelism is an easy and convenient way to attribute the cause to the symptom and confuse the two. Here is how it works.

Patient: "Doctor, my problem is _____ symptom."

Doctor: "Harry, it looks like you have _____ disorder."

Patient: "Doctor, what medication or technique will help my disorder?"

Doctor: "Harry, I suggest _____ medication and/or _____ technique to help you."

These disorders, or labels, can range from Attention Deficit Hyperactivity Disorder (commonly known as ADHD/ADD) to disorder of depression and anxiety. It could be any one of the disorders found in the medical and psychological diagnostic manuals. Either way, the implication is the same: these symptoms are the cause, and the treatment is the solution.

The medication and/or technique recommended to treat the "cause" can range from medication management to cognitive and/or behavior therapy, biofeedback, hypnosis, or any other of a myriad of techniques. The choices are many. Although these techniques can be highly effective, without treating the cause behind the symptom, their long-term effectiveness is limited (at best) to symptom management.

Unless the hidden cause is addressed, our mental health care providers (and society as a whole) will collude to squelch the taboo subject of mother-infant disconnect, calling the symptom the problem. As long as we keep diverting attention away from the cause, using labelism as a "straw man" to divert our attention away from the truth, we will never heal deeply and completely. Our collective collusion to defend against the cause is our biggest challenge to overcome.

PANEL FIVE: A VISUAL METAPHOR FOR
YOUR DEFENSE MECHANISMS

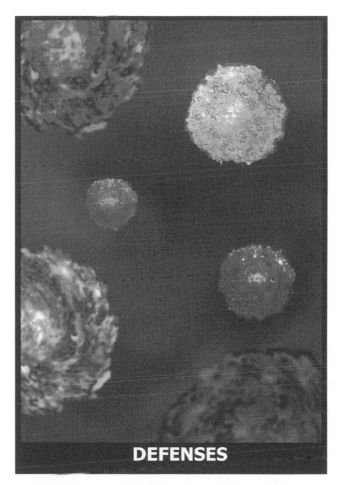

"The only defense against the world is a thorough knowledge of it." ~John Locke

Welcome to Panel Five: Defense Mechanisms. Confronting the infiltrations created by the original disconnect and freeing yourself from being imprisoned by your own defenses is the inspiration behind Panel Five. Isms have a dual nature: they can either protect you or keep you imprisoned. Your isms can be seen as your curse–by-design challenges to transform you into a healthy individual capable of healthy defense mechanisms. If all parents and parents-to-be would do the work necessary to challenge their old, destructive defense mechanisms and then heal, I believe that the next generation would be relatively symptom free.

Please study Panel Five. The orbs of Panel Five represent the duality of your isms—the positive and negative, the healthy and unhealthy, the yin and yang. Your healthy isms represent your independence, healthy boundaries, and your ability to self-sustain in the face of a toxic environment. They foster the development of your Big *I* by erecting healthy defenses to protect and preserve your original light. As you develop your healthy isms, you grow and develop the potential to share more of yourself with your loved ones, your community, and the world at large. Healthy isms, like healthy semi-permeable membranes, keep out the bad and allow the good to come through. Your healthy isms prepare you to interconnect with others in healthy ways.

The different sizes of your healthy isms represent your level of development. The different colors represent the many areas of your life (mind, body, and soul). Note that some areas of yourself may be more developed than others. For example, you may have a very developed mind but need more work on developing a healthy body.

The spongy texture of your isms represent your ability to absorb or "take in" the good around you (good emotional nutrients, love, healthy food, etc.). The more solid, impenetrable isms represent boundaries designed to shield you from emotional or environmental toxins that can harm you.

Healthy isms function to foster the development of the Big *I* by preserving your good nutrients and keeping out the bad. They keep you in a state of balance. Your unhealthy isms either block the nutrients or allow in toxins that throw you out of balance and ultimately poison you.

Notice the different sized isms suspended in the background of the toxic haze. The different sizes represent the magnitude of your defense mechanisms (both healthy and unhealthy). The greater the injury and younger you were at the time of the injury, the larger the potential will be for developing unhealthy isms. Infants who have experienced extreme forms of abuse—neglect, smothering, physical, or sexual—and/or were forced to keep secrets about their abusive past develop large isms to self-preserve. The more emotional nutrients you were given, the larger your healthy isms are.

Notice the texture of the isms. Some are spongy and penetrable. Others are more impenetrable. The more dangerous the injury and its surrounding environment, the less penetrable the isms will be. If the environment remains dangerous, the isms will grow and harden, turning malignant over time. Like cancer killing off its host, your isms will spread and destroy your emotional, physical, and spiritual well-being.

Notice the different shades of the isms and how they represent the many different styles of defenses we have already learned about (food, alcohol, other legal and illegal drugs, porn, obsessive use of phones, computers, or television).

Isms can be learned. For example, if your parents smoke, drink, or overeat, you may pick up their style of isms. You may pick a style best suited to protect you against your particular form of injury. Self-medicating with food, alcohol, and prescription and non-prescription drugs are isms effective for numbing anxiety and depression. Chronic cell phone or computer use or retreating into porn are isms that protect against intimacy.

Notice the spacing of the isms. Isolated from each other, they do not connect or interact. Isolationism creates closed systems that don't grow. Closed off and alienated from each other, they eventually get sick and die from "lack of"—lack of information, lack of interconnection, lack of stimulation, and lack of love, the most healing force known to man.

Notice the darkness in the background. The darkness is a depiction of the double dungeon of darkness from within and without. When devoid of human connection, we die mentally and physically. When devoid of the light of connection to truth, or Source, we die spiritually. Wounds incurred during infancy on into our first two to three years of life develop and harden into unhealthy defense mechanisms.

THE ROAD TO HEALTHY NARCISSISM

As you have learned from attachment theory, a child should receive the continuous care of either mother or the primary caregiver for the first two to three years of life. The outcome of the level of care during these critical years determines the development of healthy versus unhealthy narcissism.

Healthy narcissism is akin to your developed, Big *I*. Healthy narcissism is the result of "good enough" mothering, a term used by prominent psychoanalyst Donald Winnicott to describe the basic level of narcissistic emotional supplies necessary to create a healthy psyche. According to Winnicott, "good enough" mothers tend to their children with love, patience, effort, and care.

Healthy narcissism creates people with high self-esteem and emotional balance. It develops people with good boundaries and the ability for empathy and healthy relationships. Healthy narcissism creates people who are able to receive and share with others because they are fulfilled. Healthy narcissism does not create narcissistic injuries. On the contrary, healthy narcissism creates people who are self-caring, encouraging, and giving to others.

Unhealthy narcissism is the result of unmet core needs necessary for the formation of mental health. Narcissists are injured souls who did not get "good enough" mothering. As a result, they appear to be selfish and act out their injury by demeaning, devaluing, and destroying others. They act as if they are "better than" others because they feel "less than." Their behavior of superiority is a defense against their low self-esteem.

Because they make others feel as though they don't exist, narcissists have difficulty connecting and becoming truly intimate. If you take a look at the casual, "throw away" consciousness of many, we can see the "casual-ties" of narcissism: loneliness, depression, and a sense of feeling cut off from others. Rather than invest and try to reconnect relationships, many choose to break off friendships, love connections, marriages, and business associations that may have been saved had the participants given more and had the ability to care more about each other.

The degree of damage from narcissistic injury lies on a continuum. If mothering of the child is delayed for more than a year—in some cases, two-and-a-half to three years—the injury is much more severe. If mothering is delayed until after this "critical period," the child will be at greater risk of experiencing irreversible damage to the psyche. The risks continue until age five.

Psychotics and sociopaths are the irreversibly damaged. Completely devoid of either a sense of reality or empathy (sometimes both), psychotics and sociopaths are those who exhibit extreme symptoms of Human Disconnect—for example, splitting off into psychosis or committing heinous crimes. They are the ones that perpetrate the homicides and rampant public shootings and commit other horrific crimes. They are the extreme examples of the manifestation of the disconnection of the human race.

Mental and/or physical health (and un-health) develops before you are born. The foundation of healthy or unhealthy narcissism—the basis of your solid core sense of self—begins in utero.

PRENATAL CARE

Your first healthy narcissistic supplies are provided to you in utero. Naturally protected by amniotic fluid, the uterus creates the optimal environment for your healthy development. When mother does a "good enough" job, she provides you with healthy "womb service" by eating right and keeping both your and her system free from toxins (nicotine, alcohol, drugs, etc). By keeping the stress level low and shielding you from outside dangers, your in-utero experience is the first healthy defense mechanism provided to you by nature. It is your first environment for your healthy development.

If mother fails to provide you with a nontoxic, loving, and safe internal environment, your cognitive and emotional development is affected. For example, infants of mothers who smoke are often born prematurely and have cognitive, behavioral, and other developmental issues later on in life. Infants of mothers who drink or use drugs are born with fetal alcohol syndrome and/or have to suffer withdrawal symptoms from their mother's drug of choice (any drug or medication, prescription or otherwise, must be taken only if necessary and under medical supervision). Mothers under dire stress produce small-for-date infants. The effects go on.

Excellent prenatal care is the beginning of the development of healthy defense mechanisms. Healthy prenatal care offers the fetus the semi-permeable membrane of the amniotic sac that keeps out the bad and lets in the good. It's the first level of protection against psycho-viruses and other intrusions. It's the first level of the development of healthy narcissism.

POSTNATAL CARE

The next level of healthy or unhealthy narcissism is laid down in the postnatal care period. The type of attachment you form with your primary caregiver or mother during this critical period determines the health or un-health of your core physical and emotional self.

As you may recall, secure attachment can lead to the development of a solid core sense of self. Good mother-infant bonding—consisting of consistent skin to skin contact, eye contact, breast milk and unconditional love in the form of infant-centered parenting, without significant attachment breaks—creates good physical healthy, high self-esteem, healthy cognitive development, and balanced emotions. Insecure attachment can lead to low self-esteem, unbalanced emotions, difficulties in cognitive development, and even poor physical health. Attachment begins from the moment of birth.

Many health practitioners are not attuned to fostering attachment from the moment of birth. Some physicians cut the umbilical cord too soon and/or separate the baby from the mother by placing the baby in a nursery as opposed to allowing the baby to begin bonding immediately. It seems like medical practice and the practice of good mental health are miles apart. Unlike the animal kingdom, we as a human race have lost our primitive maternal instincts.

We need a more conscious and loving way to welcome babies into the world, and we need our professionals to support us in doing so. Some health practitioners make it a priority to place the baby on mother's belly and allow the umbilical cord to stay intact until it stops throbbing. Most parents don't speak up after labor and delivery, allowing the medical practitioners to do as they wish because they don't want to "upset" the doctor or the nurse.

FATHER'S ROLE IN PREVENTING POSTPARTUM DEPRESSION

The role of the father in the prevention of postpartum depression is by far underestimated. "Father", a term designated to define the individual who functions as secondary caregiver (biological or otherwise), is extremely important in providing the unconditional love mother needs in order to be a generous "giver" to her newborn. After the exhausting birthing process and beyond, mother needs more support than ever before.

Although hormone changes accompany the post pregnancy period, there is no doubt in my mind that father plays an integral part in preventing mother from "emotionally falling through the cracks" of postpartum depression. By creating a loving and supportive environment, he can provide her the emotional nourishment she needs to be a better nurturer to their infant. By helping her with the baby and making her feel beautiful, special, and appreciated, he supports her emotional well-being; he is nurturing the nurturer. As he bonds with the baby also, he becomes part of the family attachment system.

When father fails to uphold his emotional responsibility, mother can more easily fall through the cracks into postpartum depression. Already hormonally triggered, the lack of love and support from her partner can push her over the edge. Single mothers, especially those without supportive partners and loving extended families, experience the most difficulties. It is challenging for mother to give the infant the care that it needs when she isn't getting the care that she needs.

Research proves again and again that fathers are immensely important to a child's life. Men raised without fathers often have a hole inside of them, an emptiness, and a sense of loss. Some say they aren't sure how to be a man and a father. Women raised without fathers often sell themselves short by bonding with inappropriate men (or partners) in an effort to find "daddy." Fathers, as well as mothers, give their children a sense of value and set the bar for their children's sense of self-worth. A strong parental team creates the necessary pillars for children to establish security and grow.

THE FIVE HAVES OF HEALTHY NARCISSISM

If all goes well during the first phase of life, healthy isms translate into healthy narcissism. The high self-esteem that comes with this territory allows us to enjoy the five "haves" of a fully functional human being: mental, physical, intellectual, financial, and spiritual health. Your "haves" not only contribute to your own well-being but also become your potential to contribute to others. The more you have, the more you have to give to others, allowing you to more frequently reveal the light in the world.

GROWING YOUR HEALTHY ISMS

Developing a healthy sense of self is a life's journey. To grow your Little *I* and manifest your Big *I*—or healthy self-esteem—is a daily process. Growing your healthy isms is not simple, but the concept is. Developing healthy internal boundaries helps you to screen out toxins (toxic people, toxic foods, environmental toxins, toxic messages, and anything that takes away from your Big *I*). Putting up boundaries against things that interfere with your spiritual growth helps you stay on your path.

Michelle Continued.

In the process of healing or "letting go" of toxic isms, I want to refer back to Michelle, the princess of the double dungeon of darkness. With no healthy blueprint for relationships, she had no concept of what a healthy or unhealthy ism looked like. As we started distinguishing between the two, Michelle started to shift out of her old defenses and into new ones. She reported the following Panel Five experience:

I began to see the correlation between my isms and my wounds. I began to connect the dots between my mistakes, my addictions, my bad choices, and how I defended against them. I hit an "aha" moment when I realized that I had been duped into thinking that I was the reason for all the mess in my life up to this point.

Dr. Judy sat across from me as tears of remorse streamed down my face. So that explains it: My bad isms were just that, the bad news of my core wounds. I felt equipped to continue my process of letting them go. While this didn't erase my pain, I was willing to look into the hole in my soul that the isms were protecting. I looked into the dark void and jumped! I felt like I was "free-falling" my way out of the old and into the new. As I free-fell, I began to see the isms in front of me and how they protected my wound on the one hand and hurt me on the other.

As I looked further into the wound, I began to differentiate between the good and the bad, the isms that serve me and those that hurt and limit me. Later that week I started to let go of unhealthy relationships and started cleaning my house, paying my delinquent bills, eating better, and exercising more. My work began to improve, my cash flow increased drastically, and my relationship with my parents got stronger.

I noticed that my boundaries got healthier, more discerning. In this process of letting go of the old, I felt vulnerable and in unfamiliar territory. I sought healthy pillars so that I could have the support to begin to grab onto healthier isms. My pillars were Dr. Judy, conversations with my now empathetic mother, healthier lifestyle choices, professional relationships, and God. I used my healthy habits to support my "parachuting." As I fell further into my darkness, I began to see some light.

Remember to evaluate your thoughts, feelings, and habits carefully and choose only those that enhance your healthy sense of self. Thoughts that generate fear, doubt, judgment, shame, and blame diminish your Big *I*, or healthy sense of self. By recognizing your negative core beliefs, you can dismantle them on a regular basis so that you don't have to defend against them with your unhealthy isms.

By leading a healthy lifestyle consisting of good habits such as regular exercise and a healthy diet, you not only strengthen your body but also make it more resilient to disease. Through prayer and meditation, you can do what our spiritual messengers have been doing for many years: connecting to Source and sharing your unconditional love for yourself with others.

FROM *ISMS* to IT IS

How we were parented is not personal. I often tell my patients, "It is what it is." The multigenerational transmission process of psychopathology creates generations of injured parents who typically never take the time to heal themselves before having children of their own. When you see the process objectively, it makes it easier to say, "Let's start here, with me."

The most challenging aspect of working with patients is helping them understand that dealing with mother-infant disconnect and father-infant disconnect is distinctly separate from blaming mother and father. An even more difficult challenge is helping my patients break down their defense mechanisms and express the emotions contained within them. As I learned, you can't take away a person's unhealthy defense mechanisms until they learn healthy more constructive ones. Panel Six—Breakdown/Breakthrough is where all the suppressed feelings contained within the isms finally find self-expression and make room for the new paradigm.

Remember that most people don't want to tread on "emotionally dangerous" grounds to "go there" and self-express. Most would rather find a new way of defending or, better yet, staying with their old *isms*. Most don't want to journey through Panel Six and deal with the original wound or cause.

THINK LIKE A SHRINK: CONNECTING THE DOTS

- Symptoms are clues that point to the cause of the wound.
- Defense Mechanisms temporarily alleviate symptoms but eventually break down.
- The cause of the wounds occur at an early age, before you are consciously aware.
- Healthy narcissism is a result of good parenting. It develops when emotional needs are met.
- Unhealthy defense mechanisms stop you from growing. Escaping their unconscious hold on you allows you the freedom to...

Be The Cause® of better outcomes for your life!

PANEL SIX

THROUGH THE PROCESS: DECODING

BREAKDOWN~BREAKTHROUGH

"I need this old train to break down,
Oh please, just let me please breakdown!"
~Jack Johnson

True healing cannot begin until the feelings related to the original cause of all psychopathology—mother-infant disconnect—are exposed and authentically expressed. The maladaptive defense mechanisms designed to shield you from painful and long suppressed emotions from the past must eventually break down; they can only *defend* in symptom form for so long. Although my patients dread confronting the *cause*, they instinctively know that taking the psychological risk of expressing the anger and hurt behind mother-infant disconnect (and *all* significant disconnects) can lead to profound breakthroughs in their healing.

Claire took part in helping her daughter Hazel heal her separation anxiety by directly participating in her therapy. Most people are not as fortunate. Either their parents are deceased, emotionally absent, too injured, and/or unwilling to help their children heal. Fortunately, parents don't need to be present for healing to take place.

Confronting cause requires courage and honesty. Healing requires self-reflection, self-correction, and understanding that you are not the cause of Part One of your life. Healing requires taking responsibility for being the cause of Part Two. In this section, you will learn more about how people heal.

PANEL SIX: A VISUAL METAPHOR
FOR YOUR BREAKDOWN/ BREAKTHROUGH

BREAKDOWN/BREAKTHROUGH

Welcome to Panel Six: Breakdown/Breakthrough. Here is where your feelings implode, explode, crash, shatter, release, and either pave the way to Panels Seven, Eight, and Nine (Paradigm Shift, Healing, and Unity), or regress back to Panels Four, Five, and Six (Chaos, Defenses, and Breakdowns). The journey *through* Panel Six is not an easy one. It is no wonder that most people spend their lives repeating Panels Four, Five, and Six.

Panel Six is another choice point, as is the dual nature of each step in your journey. The implosions and explosions of self-expression can either destroy you and others within your path or free you from your past. Your consciousness determines whether you implode, explode, self-destruct, or heal. When you are in the consciousness of the truth and self-expression, you heal both individually and multigenerationally. When you are in the consciousness of denial and self-repression, you self-destruct and destroy others.

Please study Panel Six and notice that the *isms* of Panel Five are no longer dormant. Catalyzed and fueled by emotional injury, they become activated and begin to transform into moving, torpedo-like objects. The toxic poisons contained within them either *implode*, causing harm to the self, or *explode*, causing harm to others (sometimes both). Annihilation (to self or others) is the end game of the aggressive nature of poisonous infiltrations that have gone viral.

As is the nature of all Panels, Panel Six has a yin, or positive aspect. Look intently at Panel Six and notice the light at the contact point between the *isms*. This light is a metaphor for waging war against the infiltrations—the dark and destructive consciousness that exists within yourself and between yourself and others. Here is where clash and annihilation can shift to clash and confrontation of the original wound. Here is where healing begins.

The first war is fought in the name of what Freud called the death wish, or Thanatos—the desire to end our struggle. The second war is fought in the name of the wish to live, or Eros—our desire to transform and grow.

BEHIND THE CURTAIN OF THE ORIGINAL WOUND

Recall from Panel Five, the reason we are emotionally defensive as a human race can be traced back to the original cause of all psychopathology—mother-infant disconnect. Most of us would rather face annihilation than confront our primary caregiver about the wounds they've inflicted on us. Yet, it is this painful disconnect that perpetuates our suffering and causes the illusory and negative self-perceptions we defend against for the rest of our lives.

Just as Dorothy had to face her own illusory demons and challenges as she journeyed through her Land of Oz, you too have to face your perceptual lies or illusions as you journey through yours. Just like the Wizard was the puppet master of the illusions that created Oz, so too were your parents the puppet masters that created your illusory world filled with lies, misperceptions, and misinterpretations. Like Toto, the truth dog, we are finally pulling back the veil of truth to expose the illusion-filled movie that is your life.

You already know how your defense mechanisms can wreak havoc on your life. You are very aware of how illusions distort. Before the final curtain comes down, let's look at the types of breakdowns that can occur when *cause* is not confronted directly.

DIVORCE, BREAKUPS, AND THE "REPETITION COMPULSION"

Unresolved past issues, in what Freud refers to as the "repetition compulsion," often replay within a marriage or significant relationship. Suppressed, painful emotions—stemming from the original, unhealed wound of abandonment, or any form of mother-infant disconnect—often become retriggered and get projected into the relationship. As the love bonds get stronger between couples, the emotional investment in the relationship grows, as does the fear of losing the connection. When the hurt and anger from the unhealed childhood wounds of one partner get projected onto the other, painful core beliefs—such as "I'm not loveable," or "I'm not good enough"—retrigger. As the injuries continue to be reactivated in the relationship, the love bond breaks, and toxic emotions from the past wound erupt. This eruption, or Breakdown, is the unconscious dynamic behind many breakups and divorces.

Warren Adler's book and movie, *The War of the Roses*, is a classic depiction of the aggressive nature of divorce. It's a perfect example of a couple going through Breakdown.

A young married couple, Barbara and Oliver Rose—played by Kathleen Turner and Michael Douglas, respectively—have a marriage built on superficial bonds of money, status, and societal obligations. Unable to sustain over time, the bonds break down, and the relationship detonates, releasing years of pent up aggression and lethal toxicity. In the final death scene, the couple is seen hanging from their decadent chandelier and battling out their final aggressions, their last moments of life committed to their mutual annihilation. Their classic fall from the chandelier to their death depicts their fall from grace and their sacrificing *all* in the name of "getting even."

Their story is not unique. Many relationships become a battlefield for playing out past and unresolved infiltrations. As the pressure within the relationship mounts and the stressors of life bear down on the couple, unresolved feelings can become triggered within the relationship and get projected not only onto each other but also onto the children, close family members, friends, or *anyone else* in close emotional proximity.

The clash, detonation, and devastation triggered by breakups occurs not only in romantic breakups but in breakups of friendships and partnerships as well. The level of detonation is equivalent to the level of investment—emotional, financial, and/or otherwise.

When feelings contained within the defense mechanisms reach critical mass or the clash point, a shift occurs, and the death instinct that Freud referred to as Thanatos takes over. Whether physical or emotional, the desire for annihilation can take on nuclear proportions.

What is behind the dark curtain of Thanatos? Let's take a look at the darkest of the darks—homicide, suicide, homicide-suicide and the most taboo expression of aggression towards cause of the original wound, parricide.

HOMICIDE: AGGRESSION TURNED OUTWARD

Homicide is the darkest endpoint and ultimate expression of aggression projected and turned outward towards others. Homicide has reached epidemic proportions. Every year there are approximately 6.2 homicides per 100,000 people worldwide. Homicide can manifest as a crime of passion directed against a loved one, as an anonymous drive by shooting, or as a mass public shooting in a school, movie theater, or other public place.

How does aggression turn to murderous rage? Why do these feelings get projected onto others? Where do these feeling originate from—what is the *cause?* In order to understand the origins of massive aggression turned outward, let's go back to Panel One and backtrack to the original wound of mother-infant disconnect.

As you learned in the previous chapters, the wounds from Panel One grow into the defense mechanisms of Panel Five. When massive original injuries are left unresolved and unreleased—or worse, if physical and/or emotional abuse continues—a point of critical mass is reached. Defense mechanisms, no longer able to hold the aggressions in check, detonate, annihilating those in their wake.

SUICIDE: AGGRESSION TURNED INWARD

Suicide is the darkest endpoint and ultimate expression of aggression turned inward against the self. Extreme and chronic childhood neglect and abuse— the most severe form of mother-infant disconnect—is the basis of aggression turned inward. When there is no one to mirror unconditional love and offer kindness and empathy in dark times, there is nowhere to turn *but* inward. Unfortunately, the "inward" of an infant is not developed enough to offer him or her enough emotional support needed to thrive.

The frustrations of unmet past and current needs create toxic, aggressive, and unexpressed feelings which, over time, turn against you, break you down, and destroy you. Trapped in a double dungeon of unmet needs, suicide becomes an option as an escape route from this emotional hell.

According to the World Health Organization, suicide rates have increased by 60% worldwide in the last 45 years. Each year approximately one million people commit suicide, a global mortality rate of one death every 40 seconds. By 2020, the rate of death will increase to one every 20 seconds. Over 90% of these deaths are associated with depression or substance abuse (or both). The other 10% are most often linked to the loss of a loved one, loss of money, or disassociation from one's community. *All* of this pain and suffering is a result of Human Disconnect.

Peter
The Unexpressed Man

"Peter," age 45, suffered from an anxiety disorder and frequent panic attacks. When he was a young boy, his mother would smother a pillow over his mouth whenever he *dared* to cry, telling him to "stop it!" Raised with constant criticism and suppression of his feelings, Peter was never allowed to say what he felt. Over time, his inner and unexpressed rage grew to unmanageable proportions. Not even a heavy arsenal of psychotropic medication was effective enough to shield him from his emotional pain.

Therapy after therapy, psychiatrist after psychiatrist, Peter was unable to release the emotional pain that ate away daily at the core of his being. There were times when he became so despondent that he would stop eating. He literally whittled down into a wisp of a human being.

When Peter tried to express his feelings to his mother, she insisted that he get more medication to manage them. Peter complied by upping the dosages of his arsenal of defense mechanisms—the bottles of anti-anxiety, anti-depressant, and "anti-feeling" prescription medications that stopped working for him long ago.

Although he tried to redirect his chronic and mounting anxiety into sex, exercise, and even humor, he finally turned the toxic feelings that never got directly expressed to *cause*, against himself. Peter went to a public shooting range and shot himself in the head. He died a few hours later.

HOMICIDE-SUICIDE:
AGGRESSION OUTWARDS AND INWARDS

The names and faces may change, but the age-old theme remains the same. Crimes of passion are some of the most horrific crimes known to mankind. Defined by rage, uncontrollable jealousy, obsession, and revenge, the perpetrators tend to be possessive, domineering, controlling, lonely, paranoid, and depressed individuals. Often catalyzed by breakup or divorce, the woman, for example, who tries to end the relationship is viewed as the source of pain. To end the pain and gain control, the man (in this example) murders her.

The couple from *The War of the Roses* is a depiction of a fictional crime of passion. Unfortunately there are many cases that are all too real. When a weak core-self, injured at *cause*, is re-injured by a breakup, reactions can easily escalate into domestic violence, sometimes culminating in murder-suicides.

Murder-suicide is a dramatic and violent event in which a person—almost always a man—commits one (or multiple) murders, and then shortly after, commits suicide. What makes these acts particularly disturbing is that they often involve a family with children.

The Violence Policy Center in Washington estimates that 1,000 to 1,500 people die from murder-suicide annually. In over 90% of the cases, men are the perpetrators. In a recent Center for Disease Control survey, one in four of 9,000 women said that were attacked by their husbands or boyfriends. Knowing no bounds, an enraged father can buy into the belief that the entire family is better off dead, targeting not just the woman but the children as well. Women, on the other hand, usually target the children, rarely aiming aggression at the man.

Unemployment, foreclosure, health problems, and other stressors can trigger the homicidal individual's damaged core sense of self, detonating defense mechanisms that can no longer contain toxic and unexpressed feelings. While half of all marriages end in divorce, some end with two funerals instead.

PARRICIDE

Parricide, or the act of a child killing their parents, is an almost daily occurrence in the United States. The typical killer is an abused and neglected white male with meager financial resources, a limited education, and few to no skills. Typically, they have no history of severe mental illness or extensive delinquent behavior.

According to Paul Mones, Los Angeles-based attorney and author of *When A Child Kills,* over 90% of parricide offenders have been psychologically abused by one or both parents and have witnessed the abuse of other family members in the household as well. The children's parents, also victims of sexual and/or verbal abuse, re-create past multigenerational conditions of abuse at home. Living in an intolerable home environment and fearful of living in a dangerous and intolerable street environment, these children feel that the only way out of their intolerable family condition is to turn their murderous rage against their parents and kill them.

FEAR OF CONFRONTING CAUSE

Although few people actually kill their parents, the desire to kill our parents is a common theme in the hearts and minds of the human race. Ever hear someone (or even *you*) think or utter the words, "I wish my mother or father would drop dead?" Thinking those thoughts, let alone *saying* them, can evoke feelings of shame and guilt. Looking deeper into why we think and feel this way is even more frightening because it brings us closer to dealing with the pain of the original wound.

There are many valid reasons people want to avoid confronting *cause*. Some of these reasons are fear that they will hurt their parent's feelings, that they will risk the relationship they already have, that if they risk becoming vulnerable, they will not feel heard and empathized with yet again. In many cases their fears are not unfounded. Many parents don't want to take responsibility for the injuries they may have caused their children. Many would rather defend their harmful actions—even if unconscious and uninformed—than take responsibility and accountability for being the *cause* of their children's mental un-health.

Driven by guilt, shame, and blame, they would rather defend themselves and re-injure their child than take personal responsibility for their role in causing injury. The message, yet again: I must protect *me* before I protect *you*.

Many parents proverbially throw their children under the bus and cancel appointments right before their children are about to express past hurts. Many opt for "symptom management therapy" or psychotropic medication to "numb" their children's symptoms instead of choosing to help them truly heal.

What many parents and even many professionals don't understand—or perhaps don't *want* to understand—is that in most cases, symptoms are a direct result of mother-infant disconnect. How can a child learn to pay attention and "think" clearly and calmly when living in a chaotic, abusive, stressful home environment? By labeling them with Attention Deficit (Hyperactivity) Disorder (ADD or ADHD), parents and others can conveniently point their finger at the problem-child—protecting the problem-parent(s)—and deny seeing their symptoms as reactions to the *real* problem.

How can a child who was abandoned or disconnected from "too soon" avoid being triggered by separation? By labeling them with Separation Anxiety Disorder, parents and the community can once again divert the attention off of *cause* and on to the problem-child. In this case, labeling becomes yet another ism—a defense mechan*ism* against expressing anger at *cause*. Labeling continues to spare the parents and hurt the child.

Emotional wounds cause us to turn inward, toward our pain. When we are busy licking our emotional wounds, it is difficult for us to cope with life and live in the moment. As my patients connect the dots between their symptoms and *cause*, as they confront and express the hurt and anger that lay buried and contained within their defense mechanisms, the symptoms "miraculously" begin to subside.

Defaulting to symptom management techniques or offering organic or genetic explanations of the origins of psychopathology puts us at the *effect*, not the *cause*, of the outcome of our lives. Looking to nature (versus nurture) is not enough.

ETHICS AND CAUSE

When we are busy either defending ourselves or licking our emotional wounds, it is easy to throw our ethics and morals out the window. At times, it seems easier for some to justify their actions by lying, cheating, and/or blaming others rather than taking responsibility and working toward healing past wounds.

Ethics are of no interest and/or value to the emotionally wounded. They feel that because life has cheated them out of what is fair, they can balance the raw deal through some creative "psychological bookkeeping." Let's look at how this "bookkeeping" works:

- Stealing: If *cause* was withholding, a way to "get" is to cheat the system and "take" what should have been given.

- Lying: If *cause* was critical, a way to protect the self from being blamed is by lying and blaming others.

- Cheating: If *cause* cheated sexually, a way to protect the self from being vulnerable to being cheated on is to take control and *become* the cheater.

A powerful pathway for correcting the "ethics-gone-wrong" of psychopathology is to follow a "principles over people" philosophy. As we substitute truthful feedback for blaming, shaming, criticizing, and judging, we can hold one another accountable for adopting life-enhancing principles that bring mental health to all, evolve our ethics, and preserve the dignity of people.

CALCULATING THE DAMAGES

An integral part of expunging the wounds of childhood includes taking inventory of the damages of the original wound. Whether the damages were intentional or not, the results are the same. To illustrate this point, I often refer to the following example: if someone is hit by a truck, the damage is real and painful, regardless of whether the truck driver was at fault or not.

The damage of Human Disconnect, intentional or not, leaves a long trail of consequences. Negative core beliefs, painful physical and emotional symptoms, unhealthy defense mechanisms that hurt you and stunt your growth, bad ethics, and inability to form and maintain healthy relationships are some of the damaging consequences of mother-infant disconnect. To begin healing the disconnect, *cause* must be held accountable. Accountability begins with calculating all the ways that your life, up until now, has been damaged by the wounds of the past.

REVERSING THE DAMAGE: THE DAMAGE LIST

Expunging or exorcising the toxins requires the most difficult part of the process and most controversial part of my work: throwing the damage back to *cause*. This process is not meant to blame, shame, or criticize your parents. The process starts with a "damage list." This damage list is a list of all the damage that you incurred as a result of your childhood wounds.

Unless the parent or parents want to participate in their child's healing, they never get to see or hear the "list." It is not necessary for parents to be a part of the healing process, and many of them choose not to participate. In this instance, I become the "proxy" parent for the healing process.

The damage list is a thorough record of parental disconnects that have caused you pain and suffering and have set your life-path off course. Creating a damage list is the first step towards expressing repressed feelings and holding *cause* responsible for childhood wounds. The damage list is an integral part of healing. It takes a lot of preparation to create this truth list and "go there."

Let me remind you again that these damages are not necessarily meant to be expressed to our parents in *actuality*. For some of us, our parent/parents are deceased, or we are estranged from one or both of them. For others, this is a conversation that will never happen in a "real world" sense.

Although direct participation by one or both of our parents would be a gift of generosity (and potentially miraculous), for most of us, our parents are too old, too stubborn, too unwilling to change, and/or too in denial to own their own part in the cause.

This damage list is usually long. Once the damage list is complete, the patient and I enter into what I call the "truth conversation." This conversation is meant to complete a process I call "throwing the wounds back to *cause*." This helps my patients expunge the pain and heal quickly.

Most of my patients have a hard time with this. The guilt and shame they experience makes them revert back to excusing and protecting their parents. Over and over again, I have to remind them that compassion comes later. The Mind Map has a certain ritualistic order that must be followed: Anger before compassion. Panel Six before Panel Seven. It must go that way for healing to take place.

REVENGE FANTASIES: PSYCHOLOGICAL RETRIBUTION

Revenge fantasies are a part of the healing process. They are a form of psychological payback or retribution. The fantasies help redirect anger-turned-inward (the cause of depression and suicide) outward, towards *cause*.

Revenge fantasies help you express the raw, primitive parricidal wishes we secretly harbor within ourselves, to whatever degree we do. These fantasies are very effective ways of releasing suppressed emotional pain. Revenge fantasies are just that: fantasies. They are not suggestions to inflict damage. It is vital that when working with these fantasies there is no danger of acting them out in real life.

Revenge fantasies allow people to safely express their truth without acting out their anger and going to jail for their retaliations. My patients have shared many revenge fantasies, some of them extremely gruesome. Deep wounds can cause deep reactions to the hurt. If not released in fantasy, they are sometimes tragically acted out in reality in the form of homicide, suicide, homicide-suicide, and parricide.

I am always surprised at how my patients are both afraid and excited when telling me their unedited "truth" feelings about what happened at *cause*. As one of my patients put it, "I'm afraid to go there. But, at the same time, it sounds exhilarating." Before we begin to go into the "truth conversations," I let my patients know that we are about to reverse the process of the damage that they sponged in during Part One of their lives by "ex-sponging" their pain, allowing them to attain their freedom. Most revenge fantasies are directed against the mother, father, and/or primary caregiver.

Aaron
A Revenge Fantasy

"Aaron," age 42, was verbally and physically abused by his mother. He was constantly beaten with a stick until his legs welted then told that he was worthless. After several months of working together and identifying the "damage" of his first few years of life, he came up with the following damage list: "Because of you, I have a hard time feeling good about myself. Because of you, I have no trust in relationships. Because of you, I feel depressed and angry every day of my life."

I asked Aaron to feel free to tell me an unedited version of his revenge fantasy against his mother. I am always amazed at the amount of aggression people suppress and what comes out when permission is given to share. He shared the following revenge fantasy:

> *I am beating her head into the concrete until her brains splatter. My hands are covered in blood. I am kicking her in the womb to make sure she can never have any more children.*

After his revenge fantasy Aaron reported feeling nothing. Aaron reached a point of apathy and emptiness when he was fully expunged of his rage. In a strange way, this emptiness allowed him to have more empathy for himself. Sometimes patients are so protective of their mother that they need to start with expression of hurt and anger toward their father. The fantasies against fathers usually involve taking back power that was taken away from them, especially in the case of abused men.

Daniel
Another Revenge Fantasy

"Daniel," age 36, fantasized about throwing his father over a balcony and destroying his precious Ferrari. His father had ditched the family for another family, leaving Daniel feeling hurt, jealous, and abandoned. Destroying his father's Ferrari represented the destruction of the material possessions that were withheld from him early in life. The bloody and destructive fantasy was the first time I had heard him express any anger in his session.

When he came back the following week, Daniel told me what a great dinner he had with his father just days after his revenge fantasy. I asked him if he felt angry during the time spent with him. Daniel was surprised that he felt lighter, more connected, and more compassionate towards his father than ever before. Again, the revenge fantasy was part of Daniel's process to release his pain and anger, thus allowing him to have a better connection with his father.

THE DOMINO EFFECT OF CRITICAL MASS AND HEALING

Understand that a parent who injures their child is a parent who is injured. Healing mother-infant disconnect ideally begins with the parent healing their own childhood disconnects first. Usually the child (or adult child) comes to therapy first. Occasionally the parent(s) follow suit.

When one family member begins to heal, it often has a domino effect on other members of the family. One individual can be responsible for breaking the multigenerational transmission process of psychopathology and provide enough critical mass of courage to begin to transform the entire family.

Farah
The Binger and Purger

"Farah," a young woman in her mid-20's, courageously confronted her mother about being physically and verbally abusive. As a child, she was beaten and verbally demeaned and devalued on a regular basis. When Farah was in elementary school, her brother began to sexually abuse her. Because she couldn't confide in her unsafe and abusive mother, Farah had no place to turn but inward.

Recall that the inner world of a child, particularly an abused child, is unequipped to handle emotional reactions to trauma. To "cope," Farah began to binge and purge in an attempt to manage her repressed feelings that had manifested as depression, anxiety, and low self-esteem. The binging and purging, which turned into her diagnosed "problem" of bulimia, was her way of talking in psychological metaphor and managing her emotional pain. Caught in a web of anger at her mother and suffering from guilt and shame about the sexual abuse, binging and purging became her way of taking in the "good," soothing, fantasy mother and separating from the "bad," abusive, real-world mother. In an environment of chaos and emotional instability, food was the only thing she *could* control.

The turning point in Farah's therapy occurred when she began to understand that healing must come in layers. By metaphorically throwing up her mother and re-ingesting her all in one act, she would never be able to completely expel her suppressed emotional toxins. As she expressed her anger at her mother and brother, shared her guilt and shame about the abuse she received, and opened up about her unmet needs for love and nurturing, she began to experience a sense of relief.

As she shifted out of her victim consciousness and into the consciousness of healing, she began to express—and not repress—her angry feelings, which began to release her from the darkness of her symptoms. Because her mother was also in therapy at the time, Farah felt safe enough to confront her graciously, openly, and factually about feeling abused and unprotected as a child. Because of her mother's ability to begin to see herself as *cause*, she began to reflect on her own behavior and take responsibility for her actions (a miracle, by my patient's report).

As the circle of confronting the truth grew wider to include confronting her sexually abusive brother in a non-critical or blaming manner, her brother began to consider that perhaps he needed to seek treatment as well. Farah knew that she was transforming her family and ending a cycle of multigenerational abuse.

Once the energy behind the *isms* is released, the healing is massive and takes on its own momentum. This causes a ripple effect of family healing. The fact that the entire family then sought treatment for their own multigenerational abuse was nothing short of another miracle from my patient's perspective.

Farah used Breakdown/Breakthrough to confront, express, and heal. Instead of detonating, devastating, shaming, and blaming her family, she used truth to destroy the denial that perpetuated the family lie. Because she courageously dared to confront her multigenerational past, she broke through the family denial system and became their catalyst for healing. This confrontation was the beginning of separating herself from her infiltrated past and becoming whole.

THERAPEUTIC BREAKDOWN/BREAKTHROUGH

Sometimes *isms* neither implode nor explode and simply eat away at a person's essence. What if the defenses won't "give?" One of my chronically depressed patients complained that her defenses—in her case, isolation*ism*—was robbing her of joy. Chronic and encrusted, defense mechanisms keep out the bad as well as the good. The end result is a slow death or erosion of the self, where the light becomes so dim that neither joy nor passion nor creativity can enter.

When people continue to live in their *isms*, they need the assistance of a person like myself to crack open the shell and release the toxicity within. Therapeutic Breakdown/Breakthrough is a very effective way to detonate a defense mechanism that is harming the individual. They need to be confronted before they implode, explode, or both. Cracking open defense mechanisms is akin to detonating a bomb; often, I feel that I have to seal the area and be ready for some explosions.

Breakdown/Breakthrough is an internal war between the darkness and the light, the truth and the lies. There comes a point when the psyche becomes indignant and rejects the negative core beliefs from the past, once again retriggering you into chaos and confusion.

It is beautiful to watch the turning point when the patient expunges the lies of the past and allows for their parent(s) to psychologically die. It is here in the psychological death of the parent(s) that the wounds of the past die as well. I would like to refer back to Michelle's description of her Panel Six process:

I felt like I was pulling a bloody tampon out of my heart. The tampon represented all the hurt, lies, and wounds that were dropping an anchor into the bottom of my being and making me feel stuck. My heart felt stuffed up and clogged up with my infiltrations and couldn't let anything else good inside. Through breakdown, the time came to "exorcise" my "demons." Through several "truth talks" with Dr. Judy, directed toward mom and dad, I began to see the truth as I unloaded the pain that was no longer inside me. In one session, I remember speaking like I was 6 years old, expressing all my repressed pain and indignancy from my early childhood years.

During my process of Breakdown/Breakthrough over several sessions, my psyche and body literally started rejecting the bad. I had several psychological "breakdowns" where it felt like my brain was emptying out and looking for something to grasp onto. I didn't know what I would hold onto and feared another bad core belief would consume me.

As I emptied out the pain, I was afraid that I would be left with a new hole in my soul because I feared that the emptiness would be filled with new infiltrations. With each truth talk I did with Dr. Judy, I went further down the road of no turning back. My subconscious now knew the truth as well, and everything about me began to reject the lies and wanted to get it all out. This resistance, or confusionism, manifested itself as intolerable pain in my body. I demanded of myself to be set free.

The day I pulled the "tampon" out of my heart, I literally showed up to Dr. Judy's with a severe cramp in my chest that had me bed-ridden for two days prior. It was as if my body went into anxiety over having to finish letting go of all my pain. It is to no surprise that my muscular cramp was symbolically right around my heart center. I consulted with an urgent care physician who confirmed my symptoms were muscular and anxiety-induced. My heart was psychologically and emotionally cutting off the anchor and in a bit of panic to be set free. The biofeedback of my body was letting me know it was time to let go.

Dr. Judy acted like a surrogate mother to my final Breakdown/Breakthrough so that I could safely let go of all the bad information. She reassured me that letting go of all the bad along with the attachments that came with it, including the good, would "cleanse" me of my pain and free me by releasing it. I remember being reluctant to face "dad," whom she role-played for me. She gave me a kind nudge, "Then pay me and you can walk out of here with your pain." I preferred to stay and kick the pain goodbye.

I did my final truth talk, and toward the end of my intense cathartic release, my physical pain began to subside. I released the relationships that represented my captivity and was now free. And empty. Dr. Judy explained that my hole was now a blank slate for re-creation. My heart was now open. Because of my vulnerability, Dr. Judy encouraged me to take a little break from the world and give myself some space to heal and trust myself. I chose to be open to receive and be re-filled by an unconditional love from a higher source. I specifically found my faith in looking to letting go and letting God. This time also allowed me to process the release I just had in a healthy, safe way. I was essentially allowing in a better blueprint and new encoding, beginning my connection with my Big I.

DON'T SHOOT THE MESSENGER

Part of my job as a psychologist is to guide my patients to clash with and challenge their perceptions and core beliefs. An important part of my work centers around helping them get to *cause* so that they can express negative emotions about their family of origin and heal. At times, patients, parents, or both want to avoid the "truth conversation" and choose to get rid of me rather than confront the still taboo notion of *cause*.

Many parents are not prepared for the "truth conversation," and because of this, much of the confrontation has to take place in "role play," with me substituting for mother, father, or primary caretaker. In this role play, I stand as **"enlightened witness"** to the trauma that my patients have experienced, able to understand the insanity of the situation. This in and of itself is very healing because they have someone to mirror the fact that they are not actually crazy but have been made to believe they are crazy. I want to emphasize again that the original injurer doesn't have to be present in order for healing to take place.

Many times, mother is already deceased, absent, or simply not emotionally available to have the conversation. Sometimes parents avoid the **"truth conversation"** and sabotage my patient's ability to heal because, again, they don't want to take responsibility for the damage they caused. Often they refuse to come for therapy and do the necessary preparation to become part of the healing process. I then have to be the surrogate mother or father for my patients to process their feelings. Even when they want to shoot me down, I can't allow them to kill the messenger. The poison has to come out.

YOU YOU YOU:
THE WORD THAT CAN CAUSE BREAKDOWNS

One little word that can trigger emotional explosions or breakdowns is a little word we use all the time: *You*. You is often perceived as an attack word because it is either used to criticize another or tell others what they should or shouldn't do. For example: "You always…you never…or you should." Even when well intentioned, sentences that begin with the word "you" tend to be experienced as shaming, blaming, criticizing, or judging. Because the "you" word triggers defenses, it is wise to avoid using it, especially at the beginning of a sentence.

When the "you" word is used with individuals who have a fragile sense of self, it is felt as intrusive and finger pointing. The more emotionally injured the individual, the less they can tolerate the "you" word.

DEATH: THE FINAL BREAKDOWN/BREAKTHROUGH

Death is the final breakdown of all defenses. As death draws nearer, priorities seem to shift toward what is most important: connecting to our loved ones. As our senses begin to shut down even more, we draw inward and begin to let go of the physical world. The final clash is between Eros and Thanatos—life and death. Death is the ultimate cleansing of all our wounds, when we "let go" and return to the light of Panel One.

When our physical life dissolves, the energy contained within us is returned to Source. It is here that the final remnants of the darkness of our infiltrated past cease and move to the blank slate, or "no-thing" state. The Big Bang cycle of life renews: creation, destruction, and ultimately the paradigm shift into a higher state of consciousness or being.

You have now arrived at the end of your journey *through*. In celebration, you can now look forward to moving past your Little, infiltrated *I*, and into the earned light of your Big *I—to* compassion, life purpose, and unconditional love, the most powerful healing force known to man.

Together we have learned about the cause of our wounds, the painful reactions to them, and their embedding into our DNA in the form of our negative core beliefs. We have watched our breakdown into chaos and our reaction to it by creating defense mechanisms to shield and protect us. We have introspected on our present conditions and created a damage list to inventory our afflictions.

THE "TRUTH CONVERSATION"
BLACK ROSES MOTHER'S DAY

Cindy and Roberta Continued.

"In our struggle for freedom, truth is the only weapon we possess."
~The Dalai Lama

In order to experience an impending therapeutic "Breakdown/Breakthrough" safely and most effectively, I had to prepare both Cindy and Roberta for the "truth conversation." I started in a private session with Roberta, who was quite scared but willing to go all in to help Cindy.

"Roberta," I began, "first let me thank you for agreeing to be part of this process. I admire you. Your courage and eagerness to do this for your daughter is the greatest blessing you could ever give her—the gift of healing. This will completely fulfill your duties of mothering that you missed out on because you didn't know a better way at the time."

Roberta became emotional. "I want you to be prepared for what is going to happen on *Black Roses Mother's Day*," I began.

"Next week, you and your daughter Cindy are going to sit down in this room together. We now all agree that the purpose of this process is to break the old dysfunctional mother/daughter bond that imprisoned Cindy in her double dungeon of darkness.

"With mutual respect in your hearts, you will sit across from one another. When Cindy is ready, she will face you and begin speaking her truth from the bottom of her heart. She will start with, 'Because of you ...' and what pours out of her at this point will be all of the poison, pain, toxins, pollutants, defense mechanisms, and injuries of her life. They will all be directed at you, not to blame or shame, but to express the full truth of her feelings.

"You will sit and listen. You will allow Cindy to vomit up all her truth and you will receive that poisonous bile without speaking. When Cindy is completely finished, you will simply tell her, 'Thank you for sharing your truth.' If Cindy requires anything else from you, she will tell you. Then I will thank you, and Cindy will decide what happens next. Do you understand?"

"Yes," Roberta said, her lips trembling. "It's all going to be okay," I assured her. The calendar was marked for the day.

In the meantime, I met with Cindy to prepare her as well for *Black Roses Mother's Day*. "Cindy," I began, "we are going to go through a little rehearsal process for the big day. Your mother is allowing herself to be the target for all of your pain. She has come into this willingly, with a desire to help you heal. She urgently wants to relieve the burden that she herself put on you in your infancy and childhood."

"This will not be the time to candy-coat what you truly want to say. I have prepared your mother to receive everything that you need to share. There will be water and plenty of tissues, and we can take breaks as often as you like. But understand Cindy, this is your golden opportunity to release all of the bottled up poison you have carried around for so many years.

"You will sit in my chair and when you are ready, you will face your mother and begin, 'Because of you ...' Then, you will release each entry of your damage list one by one. There will be no need for you to hold back. You can take as much time as you want. You can stop when you need to. You can also talk about your own relationship isolation from your daughter, Kate. Your mom will not respond unless you ask her a specific question. Try to stay with the *Because of You* list so that you can purge every last drop of poison. When you are finished, your mom will thank you, and then you will decide what you wish to do next. Do you understand?" Cindy nodded. "Do you have any questions?" I asked. She shook her head "no." We confirmed the date and time.

The whole family was nervous but excited about the big day. I felt sort of like an exorcist, preparing to face the evil spirit of multigenerational darkness with prayer and hope. All of us knew our roles and were eager to play them.

The mood was subdued but not melancholy. We began by reciting The Lord's Prayer: *"Our Father, which art in heaven..."* Next, we set our intention to "express the repress" and clean the past so that there could be release, healing, and an opportunity for a new beginning. I told Cindy to sit with her legs uncrossed, look her mother in the eyes—eye to eye, or *I to I*—and allow herself to be very vulnerable. Cindy began as Roberta sat and listened:

Because of you, Mom, I don't feel important. I never came first. I'm shut off, desensitized. I've been so angry for as long as I can remember. I have no voice. I don't know how to move forward and live my life. I have wasted so much time...

The exasperation and outrage came pouring out. At one point, I asked Cindy to stop and allow her tearful mother to process the pain. "Think of each piercing-through-your-heart stab," I offered Roberta, "as a beautiful opportunity to take on your daughter's pain and repair the relationship." This sentiment allowed Roberta to welcome this difficult communication.

As I witnessed the release of emotions, I noticed Cindy become more calm and confident. At the end of the session, Roberta thanked her daughter for sharing her truth. We concluded with an acknowledgment of the courage it took for both mother and daughter to enter into the "truth conversation."

Cindy decided to leave the session before her mother so that she could process her feelings alone. Roberta appeared to need comforting so she stayed with me for a while to debrief.

It is extremely important to allow for this breathing space between mother and daughter. Time and patience provide opportunity for the separation and individuation process, sowing the seeds of a healthier relationship.

Black Roses Mother's Day shined the truth-light on the unconscious and made it conscious. By decoding her past and releasing the pain, Cindy was free to move into the future with a clean slate, a fresh sense of hope, and an unsullied perspective on life, love, and possibility.

> *When we quit thinking about ourselves and our own self-preservation, we undergo a truly heroic transformation of consciousness.* ~Joseph Campbell

As we move forward to Panel Seven, let us note that the chasm from Panel Six to Panel Seven is a leap that may not be achieved on the first try. It may take several attempts before you are able to clear that final hurdle. Every practice jump is preparation towards triumph. In the end, you *will* be victorious. When all is said and done, you *will* be free.

THINK LIKE A SHRINK: CONNECTING THE DOTS

- Symptoms are clues that point to the cause of the wound
- Defense Mechanisms temporarily alleviate symptoms but eventually break down.
- The cause of the wounds occurs at an early age, so they are unconscious.
- Healthy narcissism is a result of good parenting and emotional needs being met.
- Unhealthy defense mechanisms stop you from growing. Freeing yourself from their unconscious hold on you allows you to...

Be The Cause® of better outcomes for your life!

PANEL SEVEN

TO THE SOLUTION: RECODING

PARADIGM SHIFT

"People are like stained glass windows; they sparkle and shine when the sun is out, but when the darkness sets in, their true beauty is revealed only if there is a light within."
~ Elizabeth Kubler-Ross

As you heal from your infiltrated past, you may notice that your psychoperceptual lens is beginning to clear. Less vulnerable to viewing yourself and the world around you through a cracked lens of distorted lies and illusions, you are better able to shift your vision and view life through your truth lens.

Now more aware of how your childhood wounds created a world filled with psychopathology and pain, you are better equipped to stop the perpetuation of these psycho-viruses, reboot the system, and create a much more sustainable life. Re-creating your life through this new, clear-sighted lens is the inspiration behind Panel Seven.

Because you've done the work of confronting the *cause* and releasing the poisons from your childhood wounds, your ability to see the choices in front of you and the consequences of their outcome will be greatly enhanced. Clearing away the past is the catalyst to your paradigm shift. Panel Seven represents the coming together of the healthier and more healed aspects of yourself. The logo for my Be The Cause System is a symbol of that unification—mind, body, and soul. It is also a symbol of the synergy and paradigm shift that is created when this unification occurs.

PANEL SEVEN: A VISUAL METAPHOR FOR YOUR PARADIGM SHIFT

PARADIGM SHIFT

Please study Panel Seven. Panel Seven is a visual representation of your paradigm shift into healing. As your healthier defense mechanisms continue to take over the function of your unhealthier ones, you may notice a new sense of wholeness beginning to emerge. The light in the center represents the rebirth of your Big *I*, that light within that was always your birthright. Once eclipsed by your dark, unconscious, infiltrated past, your wiser, healthier, more conscious and enlightened self is now more able to break through and claim victory over your struggles.

Welcome to Panel Seven: the Paradigm Shift. No longer in the double dungeon of darkness, you are now able to be more *causal* and create a better outcome for Part Two of your life. Panel Seven is the death of the old paradigm and the commencement of the new. It symbolizes a shift in your consciousness.

Please take a moment to acknowledge yourself for shattering the lies and illusions of your past and humbly acknowledge that the work of continually exposing them is a lifetime process. Take a moment to appreciate your journey *from* your unconscious past and *through* the challenges of your breakdown. Hindsight can offer you a better appreciation of the curse-by-design challenges that motivated you to break down your old, unsustainable system. Your old, dysfunctional system needs to die before you can step into the light of Panel Seven.

You have identified the original wound, released the pain, and redirected the repercussions back to the *cause*. You courageously expressed the suppressed truths that backfired in the form of suppression and implosions and/or aggression and explosions. Because of your courage to tell the truth, the secret is out; the taboo has lifted.

It all began in Panel One when you traced back your present psychopathology to its root cause: the initial mother-infant disconnect. It is perhaps astounding to discover that as a tiny infant seeking the fulfillment of your most basic and essential needs you were infiltrated by the flaws, idiosyncrasies, and errors in attunement of your primary caregiver, leaving you feeling *less than* in value.

Armed with this new information, you then witnessed in Panel Two your own infant reactions to this initial wounding and the *failure* of your primary caregiver to adequately supply your critical emotional, physical, and/or psychological needs. You also learned about the crucial role your father played in the development of your sense of self-worth, being the first model of life outside of you and your mother. As an infant/toddler, you observed yourself forced to turn inward in attempt to cope with the injuries of those vulnerable years and observed how you entered the double dungeon.

In Panel Three, you started to comprehend how the consequence of your specific injuries and your distinct responses to them produced a *negative core belief* in the fiber of your being. You saw how this *distorted lens* of self-perception became embedded into your psyche, just like DNA.

You became conscious of the fact that you were *encoded* with a sense of self-value equivalent to the level of psychological and emotional nourishment you received throughout those childhood years. You began to understand how the *you of then* became the *you of now* and how your core belief shaped your psyche.

This journey back into your childhood then exposed you to the idea of a *precipice*—a critical choice point that propelled you into a chasm of confusion and trepidation—and how your present day circumstances were and are a direct and indirect result of that precipice of decision. You also got an opportunity to see how the system of self-degradation and devaluing that was created in your childhood—based on the lies and fabrications that made up your negative core belief—became no longer sustainable in the light of grown-up truth and experience. You can see how the chaos that overwhelmed you then—and is still trying to overwhelm you now—was your curse-by-design opportunity for massive healthy change and renewal.

Together, we dove into Panel Four, observing the utter pandemonium caused by the breakdown of your faulty wiring. You got to watch how the *younger you* struggled through the volcanic eruption of feelings, emotions, and life events. As the *adult you*, you began to see that the chaos is still terrifying, the fears are still palpable, and the sensations are still incredibly real. Perhaps experiencing the triggering of those past feelings, you started to recognize that you can't go back to where you've been without incurring even more undesirable consequences. With this knowledge comes great power and even greater responsibility.

You also had the opportunity to make a *damage list*—an inventory of all the obstacles, difficulties, and pain that you have faced. You were asked to make this list in order to mend those childhood injuries that have manifested themselves into your present suffering.

In Panel Five, you learned that during your younger life you attempted to counter the bedlam and bewilderment with coping skills that came directly out of your impairments and harmful negative core belief. Some of these defense mechanisms were healthy and have served you quite well. Others only contributed to your preservation temporarily but eventually became antiquated and broke you down over time. As you surveyed the usefulness (or lack thereof) of your defense mechanisms, you learned that the necessity for modification and adaptation would certainly come about with or without your compliance.

In Panel Six, you witnessed another detonation of unsustainable systems as the erosion of your unhealthy defense mechanisms and their consummate effect on you either ignited an external fallout (explosion) or an internal combustion (implosion). Either way, destruction and desecration were left in their wake. You have finally arrived in Panel Seven. The Little *I*, or sick child of the sick mother and father, ultimately had to die and make room for the Big *I*.

Dr. Elizabeth Kubler-Ross talks about the stages of denial, anger, and bargaining as part of the process of letting go. If you find yourself grieving the loss of your old self, please take comfort in the fact that before you can truly forgive your parents and caretakers, you must break your final connection to your infiltrated past. The grief process is fraught with denial, bargaining, and finally, a sense of acceptance. Only when we release the hurt and anger from the past can we truly forgive, reboot, and recreate.

As you study Panel Seven, notice the light bursting through the darkness. Recall that your state of un-health was created through a perceptual illusion. As you journey *through* Panel Seven you will discover that these illusions of lies no longer need to be your guiding source. As you shift further out of your old core negative beliefs and negative states of consciousness you will be in a more powerful position to *Be The Cause* of creating a touching, moving, and inspiring consciousness that will call you to action. You are winning the war against the wounds of your past,

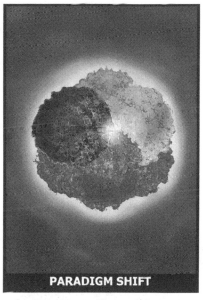

PARADIGM SHIFT

and you can now create a better outcome for Part Two of your life.

As the psycho-viruses clear out and you begin to live your life in the light, remember that the curtain or veil of illusion is just a trigger away. Please stare at the orbs in Panel Seven, noticing the light in the center of the multiple orbs. Just like the dog, Toto, who exposed the manipulations of the Wizard of Oz, you have pulled the veil of illusory lies away from your infiltrated eyes and exposed the truth.

Although your healthy *I* can serve to keep your light exposed, know that at any moment the illusory veil can come down, eclipsing the light and blocking the truth. By staying vigilant and conscious at all times, you can learn to differentiate the truth from the lies, keeping the truth exposed. With practice, this process becomes easier over time.

WHAT IS A PARADIGM SHIFT?

A paradigm shift is a new way of seeing through the lens of your new way of being. It is a radical shift in your experience of yourself and the world around you. A paradigm shift is a transformation that is permanent once experienced. You can't unlearn what you've learned.

Some people's self-esteem is so damaged that they do not believe they can ever shift. They do not believe they can ever go through the metamorphosis into a butterfly. Their bar is so low due to their limiting and negative core belief that at best they feel they can only achieve the status of a "pesky pantry moth" (once shared to me verbatim by a patient).

Think of Copernicus discovering that the earth revolved around the sun when everyone thought that it was the earth at the center of the universe. Imagine the resistance that he experienced to this new way of seeing. Imagine the challenge he was faced with when the world responded from an egocentric point of view and reacted in narcissistic "shock" that we as a human race did not take center position in our universe!

Although his instruments proved his view of Earth to be accurate (the telescope was his truth lens), it took time for everyone around him to see and accept the new facts. Copernicus experienced a paradigm shift. The world later followed suit, albeit with resistance.

THE DOLPHIN DREAM: MY PARADIGM SHIFT

I had a dream that I was in the middle of the ocean, sitting on a rock. A very kind and wise dolphin swam up, climbing onto the rock beside me. I was acutely aware that I was afforded the privilege of asking just one question from this master of wisdom. I remember feeling very pressured to come up with the "right" question, as I only had one opportunity to tap into the wisdom of this higher level being. After pondering for what felt like minutes, I asked the dolphin this: "Who rules the ocean?" The dolphin master answered, "We don't think that way. We do not dwell on who "rules" the ocean. Instead, we are interconnected."

This dream symbolizes the backbone of my Be The Cause system, even though I didn't know it at the time. It was a wakeup call to me to shift my paradigm from one of competition to interconnection. Panel Seven was born out of that dream.

Michelle Continued.

My experience through paradigm shift led me to being open to a new way of being and seeing. I considered it my "rebirth process." This part of my journey opened up many questions for me on how my process would all make sense. How would I practically apply my growth and learning in my daily life? In what ways would my psyche continue to clear out old things that I felt held me back?

The way I processed my final release of old wounds, my welcoming of what is for me, God's unconditional love and light, and my way of allowing myself and my mind to see a clear transition from who I was to who I was becoming, was through prayer, meditation, and a lot of self–care.

What made my spiritual connection during this time different from any other time in my life was that it was aligned and magnified with the growth and healing I was experiencing. My old self could never connect in this way because when I would look out into the world, all I would see looking back to me was validation of my wounds and misperceptions. Now, having grown, the new lens I was seeing through allowed me to receive more truthful information because my perception wasn't tainted like before. My old lens had lies; my new lens sought truth.

Whenever a clue came up I let it guide me to self-awareness. This left me with even more questions. If I'm not my old self, who am I? How would I feel if I was authentic in my life? What does it feel like to express my feelings, rather than the feelings I always thought would please others? How could I trust myself to make my own choices, express my own thoughts and feelings, and know that that is enough? My core belief was that I was worthless and unimportant, and I had to get better at spotting the truth.

I was "road-blocked" by a blind spot in my paradigm shift; I had always latched onto whatever temporarily seemed sturdy in my life, like a school of thought or the mimicking of a person, giving a 'carbon-copy' version of myself based on what I took from another as what I should express. How could I truly process my paradigm shift if I was yet to trust and know the mind I was shifting?

This blind spot was uncovered, and now I have my own mind to shift from and begin to see things in a new way. This doesn't mean I would know it all off the bat. I became aware and could grow from there. I began to trust my authentic self and expression as I was coming to know it. Rather than only processing through the Mind Map as a good student and patient, I could now make my transformation my own experience by seeing how I felt about it versus just going through it. I found more confidence and trust within myself and out in the world."

Helen
A Shift in Consciousness

"Helen," age 42, came to therapy because her husband and children were complaining that she was not giving enough emotional attention to them. Her son and daughter were upset about her being an absentee mother. Her husband was ready to divorce her for being emotionally neglectful.

Helen was so motivated to keep her family that she went on a mission to expose her fatal relationship flaws. She took it upon herself to ask her friends, business partner, and even children for honest feedback about her behavior. Her inner circle did not hold back. The most impactful and sincere feedback was from her son, who told her that he hates her because she never plays with him or listens to him talk about his day.

Raised by highly critical parents, Helen had internalized the critical, judgmental voices of her parents. Her constant self-evaluation left her with the conclusion and primary core belief that she wasn't "good enough." This constant self-criticism left her feeling anxious and depressed.

As she began to understand that she was treating herself as her parents treated her, she grew more indignant about having projected her parents' messages into her now almost ruined relationships. Our work was centered around turning the focus of her aggression from inward (her depression) to outward (self-expression). Our "truth conversations" about her anger towards her parents morphed into a lifting of her depression and a softening of her desire to shut down and withdraw.

During a session, she turned to me and said, "It's kind of like I'm drinking my own Kool-Aid, isn't it?" This "aha" moment was a turning point for her. From that point on, she noticed that the replayed parental messages in her head were beginning to wind down.

Her husband, however, was waiting for the other shoe to drop. As she became more emotionally available to her family, he became irate at her kindness and availability. He didn't believe that she would sustain this new behavior and thought that she was faking it to avoid losing him. Just like the world didn't believe Copernicus' world view, the world around Helen refused to believe that her paradigm shift was authentic and permanent. It took time for her family, friends, and husband to adjust to her new way of relating to them.

It is not easy to exorcise the poisonous familial messages ingrained into one's psyche. Many people are tortured with these horrific messages of shame, blame, criticism, and judgment for too long. Some believe that they need this punitive "internal parent" to whiplash themselves into discipline, thinking that they will decompensate into dysfunction if they let the messages go. When prisoners are released from jail, they oftentimes feel lost and confused when set free from their old system. Letting go of old paradigms can feel unfamiliar, un-familial, and downright threatening, even when the new ones are healthier.

Maya
Another Shift in Consciousness

"Maya," a 39 year old single mother and her two daughters—"Alana," age 10, and "Tara," age 13— came to see me for family therapy. They were constantly fighting over their possessions and tearing each other's hair out. Referring to the Mind Map, I asked the younger sister to identify the "problem" behind the behavior. Her face lit up as she pointed to Panel One and said, "It's my consciousness! I'm in a selfish consciousness."

Alana was able to see that her selfish consciousness was the cause of the breakdown of her sisterly bond. Once she and her sister were able to see how the outcome of their behavior was controlled by their consciousness, they shifted to the consciousness of sharing—a derivative of unconditional love—and resolved their conflict. By sharing consciousness, they shifted their lenses of perception, birthing new behaviors. They began sharing their clothes and jewelry and developed a sense of appreciation for each other. By tapping into their sharing consciousness, they solved the problem of "sisterly disconnect." As you can see, shifting your consciousness is the causal force that determines the outcome of your life.

SYNERGY

Synergy is what happens when we interconnect. It is the "1+1=3" phenomenon. In other words, when two people come together, a greater, third entity is created because of their affiliation with one another. Just like a magnifying glass increases the intensity of the heat, healthy synergistic relationships magnify creativity and productivity, reducing stress and workload.

When we interconnect, we can create what is known as the "whole is bigger than the sum of its parts" effect. But sometimes our synergistic attempts don't synergize. Not all interconnection is synergistic and transformational.

VAMPIRES (OR EMOTIONAL PARASITES)

Vampires (Dracula, Nosferatu, those kids from *Twilight* and *True Blood*) are mythological beings that subsist by feeding on the life essence of living creatures. They appear all throughout literature, art, and entertainment, and disturbingly enough, also in the real world. When I talk of *vampires* and *parasites*, I speak of those people in your life who pull from you, drain you, suck the very life out of you, and feed on your vitality and light. They are infiltrated souls who must, with their own darkness, deplete your luminosity in order to survive and flourish.

They are the mothers who leach from their children, reversing the role of giver and receiver. They are the narcissists whose selfishness require constant attention and stroking. They are the co-dependent individuals who, void of the nourishment of their own mother's milk, are ever hungry and thirsty for the lifeblood of others. These creatures of the night (and day) are to be avoided at all costs. They will zap your energy and take your emotional treasures for their own.

TRAITS OF AN EMOTIONAL VAMPIRE

Emotional vampires are all around you. They are often the low energy, needy, abandoned, rejected, seekers and hoarders of constant attention, nurturing, and reassurance. They are *never* satisfied.

Dr. Judith Orloff, an Assistant Clinical Professor of Psychiatry at UCLA, suggests tuning in to your physical reactions—such as a tightening in the chest, tiredness, or headaches—after interactions with certain people. This is how you can tell that you have been bitten. Don't allow yourself to fall asleep in their poppy field.

HOW TO BE A VAMPIRE SLAYER

Besides sheer avoidance, you can protect your psyche by recognizing the gradual depletion of your energy and limiting your contact with that person(s). Good boundaries are key to making sure that you are able to screen and filter them out.

Selflessness, generosity, and altruism each have their limitations. You must make a sacred commitment to protect yourself from these invaders and balance your kindness, unselfishness, and nurturing with self-protection. Your best defense mechanism is to become like a semi-permeable cell membrane, allowing in only good emotional nutrients and screening out the poisons.

INTERCONNECTION THROUGH SELF-COMPASSION

Like Helen, many people continue to replay negative messages their parents programmed them with, desperately trying to get them out of their head. Oftentimes they try to do this by self-medicating with drugs and alcohol, just so they can quiet the critical voices. Like their parents, they continue the pattern of abusing the "inner child."

Amad
Indignation as a Paradigm Shifter

"Amad," age 38, came to see me because he was suffering from alcohol abuse, gambling, depression, and anxiety. His mother continuously degraded him, telling him that she wished that he was never born. He suffered from low self-esteem and lack of trust. Most importantly, he didn't think anyone could help him get better.

Even though his mother was no longer in his life, he continued to play her broken record of demeaning and judgmental messages in his head. I see this often in my practice. The paradigm shift for them happens when they find their *indignation*. Indignation is a powerful healing force. The shift occurs when we become indignant and choose self-compassion. We shift when we choose *I* over them (our parents). When we become synergistic within the core of our being, we become whole, complete, and more *causal*.

INTERCONNECTION THROUGH RELATIONSHIPS

As you are now aware, some relationships can be healing; others are not. The first relationship with mother or primary caregiver is the first blueprint of the possibility of a healing, nourishing, growth-producing relationship. The relationship with father is the first experience of taking in nourishment from the outside world other than mother.

Our parents set the bar for relationships. If our parents were "good enough," we tend to see the world as good and safe. If our parents were injurious to us, we tend to experience the world as threatening and unsafe. We can only experience others as benevolently as we were treated. Our parents simultaneously set the bar *and* limit our ability to trust. If our primary relationships go right, we are free to Be The Cause of healthy outcomes for our life. If they don't, we become trapped in the double dungeon of darkness.

All nourishment starts from the outside in. Our relationship with mother and father is an outside-in system. When we are properly nourished and have developed a healthy core self, we can then (and only then) be able to self-sustain and survive without them. Healthy dependency leads to healthy separation and individuation. It is a fallacy to think that we don't need each other. We were born in relationship to others, and we continue to desire to relate to others. We are wired to connect!

Sociological studies and neurobiological studies continue to support the fact that mental health requires the support of community and that being isolated is dangerous to our emotional and even physical well-being. Studies show that people who lack support are more prone to stress and disease than those who have a solid community/support system around them. It is a known fact that hugging releases endorphins that buffer us from life's stressors.

Many people start with the best intentions of having a relation-*ship* and end up in relation-*sh*t*. Without doing the work of cleaning the past, their relation-*ship* ends up being a *Titanic* type relation-*ship*, headed for disaster, doomed to sink.

When the *Titanic* was built, more attention was given to the beauty and elegance of the ship than to the safety of its passengers. When the iceberg disaster occurred, there were not enough lifeboats to save all the people on board. Ships (like all relation-*ships*) that are built on weak, poor, and superficial foundations with no safety measures in place are doomed to sink. With work and relationship skills, couples can reverse this sinking process and relation-*shift* into clear sailing.

Dr. Stan Tatkin, author of a book titled *Wired for Love,* talks about a "couple bubble." A couple bubble is a term he uses to describe two people in a committed relationship who have each other's backs. Imagine if we were all couple bubbles to each other, whether it be marriage, family, friendship, business partnership, and/or community. What would be possible if we agreed to Be The Cause to enhance each other's growth? Imagine what life would be like if we could morph out of the old system of blame, shame, criticism, judgment, and all forms of negative consciousness and utilize honest, rigorous, solicited feedback to correct and evolve.

INTERCONNECTION THROUGH *THE NOW*

Eckhart Tolle, in his brilliant book, *The Power of Now,* describes how the "pain body," the collective manifestation of all the pain, misery, and sorrow you've ever gone through in your lifetime, usurps your "moment" and takes you on a journey into distractions of the past and worries about the future. Tolle, like many before him, understood the power of "now" as a portal into the moment and out of pain.

When you open your eyes to the *now,* you connect to "the flow" and become "at one" with the world. When you immerse yourself in the sounds and beauty of nature and focus your attention on your surroundings, you move into the un-infiltrated *now.*

In contrast, when you disconnect from the *now* by thinking about the past or worrying about the future, you allow for infiltrations to seep in and become activated. The power of *now* is the catalyst for paradigm shifting into being alive. The erasing of your past wounds clears the pathway to be in the *now*.

BEYOND INFILTRATIONS
(If I am not my infiltrations, *who am I* ?)

Look intently at Panel One again, into the center, beyond the shadows, to the source of light. Remember that you entered the world with a clean slate.

WHO AM I (BIG *I*)?

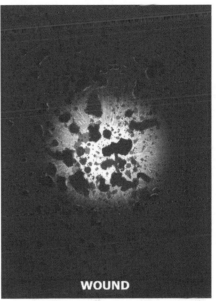

WOUND

Who are you beyond your wounds, limitations, and distorted perceptions of yourself? Ask yourself this question frequently to continue to distinguish between *who you are* as the Big, un-infiltrated *I*, and *who you are* as the Little, infiltrated *I*.

Hungarian psychologist Mihaly Csikszentmihalyi talks about being "in the flow" as a magical state of being when the creative process is on automatic and time and analytical thinking is suspended. Many creators refer to the flow as an intoxicating state of artistic bliss inspired or channeled from a source outside themselves. Rappers talk about being "in the flow" when words, beats, and music come together. Meditators refer to it as being "in the zone." When you are "in the flow" you are in the being of your *Big I*, in sync with universal flow, or Source, free from infiltrations and connected to the light.

Those who have reached the highest levels of consciousness know about the illusion of darkness and can bypass the shadows by tapping into "the flow."

Rav Shimon Bar Yochai, author of *The Book of Zohar* (The Book of Radiance), understood the distinction between the physical self and the spiritual soul-self. He buried himself in a cave to disconnect from his physical being and connect to Source. Through removing his ego and "tapping into the flow," he channeled the Zohar, the key to the deepest secrets of the universe. Rav Shimon Bar Yochai and other wisdom masters understood that we are spirits having a human experience, not vice versa. Our wisdom masters understood that our core is spiritual, not physical.

INTERCONNECTION THROUGH SOURCE

"Whether one believes in a religion or not, and whether one believes in rebirth or not, there isn't anyone who doesn't appreciate kindness and compassion." ~ Dalai Lama

When you partner with kindness, compassion, and truth, you are partnering with your authentic self, or Big *I*, and allowing yourself to grow beyond the damaging effects of your infiltrated past. When you align with the authentic expression of your higher self, you create a life that can inspire you to master your talents and share them with others.

For some, the journey to your Big *I* is the journey past your wounds and back to Original Cause, God, Universal Truth, or however you choose to define Source. Direct-connecting to Source offers us a way to heal the past and tap into the unconditional love that our parents were unable to provide.

REBOOTING THE SYSTEM

According to Himalayan tradition, everything comes from the primordial vibration of Om—all "things," including living beings, emanate from this sound. The sound of Om is known to have healing powers. The vibration of Om is described as a vibrational tuning fork bringing our soul-self in balance with Source. It is no wonder that the sound of Om is heard internationally—in the word Shal*om*, peace in Hebrew, or Sal*am*, peace in Arabic, or even the word h*om*e, a place we associate with peace and love. It is no coincidence that chanting this sound transports us into the *now*, to Source, and beyond our wounds.

Whether you choose prayer, meditation, creativity, kindness, being of service, or any and/or all of the above to connect, direct-connecting to Source allows us to co-create through wisdom and compassion and be *causal*. Our spiritually elevated messengers devoted a lifetime to prayer and meditation so that they can connect to the Source of unconditional love and share that light with others. They all seemed to know where healing flows *from*.

Cindy and Roberta Continued.
White Roses Mother's Day

When we last left Cindy and Roberta, they had just gone through the difficult emotional catharsis of *Black Roses Mother's Day*. Here is their first session together after the cathartic day:

Roberta was already in my office and seemed contemplative and a little nervous. Cindy showed up to the session in white, her t-shirt reading, "I Love Mom." Roberta smiled as she looked at her daughter's shirt. Cindy sat in my chair and began, "Mom, because of you..."

Roberta flinched, but Cindy continued, "Because of you, I am healing. Because of you, I have a second chance at my life. Because of you, I have a new relationship with you and Kate" (Cindy's 6-year-old daughter).

Roberta seemed shocked and somewhat uncomfortable with hearing these loving words. Cindy left the room. When she returned, she brought with her a dozen long-stemmed white roses that she had ordered. She gave them to her mom. We all broke down in tears; everyone was reaching for the tissues. The "tissues for the issues" were now tissues for the *healed* issues. It was one of the most rewarding moments of my career.

Through the "truth conversation," Cindy was able to free herself from her negative core belief, shatter the lies of her infiltrated past, and release herself from her childhood hostage situation. When we have the courage to confront the lies of our infiltrated past, paradigm shifts happen.

As we continue your journey into Panel Eight, keep in mind that you have done much work to finally be able to truly forgive yourself and your once-captors (mother and father) who, like you, were trapped in their own double dungeon of darkness, unable to escape their own childhood hostage situation.

Please take a moment to recognize your paradigm shift and acknowledge yourself for being the cause of your own healing. Because of me...

THINK LIKE A SHRINK: CONNECTING THE DOTS

- A Paradigm Shift is a new way of seeing through the lens of your new way of being.
- When we become synergistic within the core of our being, we can become more *causal*.
- Synergy is the "1+1=3" phenomenon.
- Being of service allows us to experience our Big *I* and pay it forward to others.
- Living life through the lens of truth creates Paradigm Shift, Healing, and Unity, while living life through the cracked lens of lies creates Chaos, Defenses, and Breakdowns.
- Which lens you choose to see through determines the direction of your life. Choosing to see through the truth lens allows you to…

Be The Cause® of better outcomes for your life!

PANEL EIGHT

TO THE SOLUTION: RECODING

HEALING

"Your genetics load the gun. Your lifestyle pulls the trigger."
~Mehmet Oz

Your psychological cancer is past remission. The poison has been drained. The fissures removed of their infection are now healing. You are now in a stronger position to "recode" yourself with a more accurate, life-affirming, and positive core belief.

Research from the field of epigenetics tells us that rather than set in stone, the expression of our DNA is malleable, meaning that we are coded to have the ability to recode! This is powerful information and very profoundly optimistic about our ability as a human race to transform ourselves.

As you let go of the old coding, you can now Be The Cause of selecting the new life-sustaining psycho-DNA into the fiber of your being. Think of this recoding process as a kind of repair, or re-parenting of the self, leading to a rebirth after the "apocalypse" of Panel Six. This new, more functional self can now create a healthier Part Two outcome for your life.

Because health begets health, this new information will begin to replicate healthier psycho-DNA—the kind that will not make you "psycho." The new encoding is your reward for freeing yourself from the past and giving it all back to *cause*. As you re-code yourself and become a part of a powerful healing chain, you can choose to evolve up the ladder of challenges, illuminating the pathway of healing for others.

Judy Rosenberg Ph.D.

REPAIRING THE "PSYCHO" DNA

According to Alan Sroufe, Ph.D., the brain continues to remodel itself in response to experiences throughout our lives. The brain is malleable, or neuroplastic. Relationships can stimulate neuronal activation and even remove the synaptic legacy of early social experience. Dr. Murray Bowen calls this phenomenon the "multigenerational transmission process." The verdict is in; the case for attachment theory passes with flying colors.

According to Dr. William Harris, Professor of Child Psychology in the Institute of Child Development and adjunct professor of psychiatry at the University of Minnesota:

The brain continues to remodel itself in response to experience throughout our lives, and our emerging understanding of neuroplasticity is showing us how relationships can stimulate neuronal activation and even remove the synaptic legacy of early social experience...In this way, clinical practice can use the power of our attachment relationships to cultivate deep and lasting change throughout the lifespan and even stop the transmission of disabling early experiences across the generations.

Our synaptic connections and our brain chemistry are a clear example of the mind/body connection. When we begin to heal these disconnects, everything seems to flow better.

Recall the example of an imaginary lemon creating saliva in your mouth. If an *imaginary* lemon can create *real* saliva, imagine how our thoughts can affect our brain chemistry and impact our emotions. The brain is the center of our psychopharmacological laboratory. When we are emotionally disconnected *from*, our thinking, or cognition, is negatively impacted.

As we reconnect our emotions, our neuro-synapses heal, and we create better pathways for transmitting healthier neurochemicals. As we mend our minds through mending our interpersonal connections, we can experience more emotional stability and healthier thinking.

As you heal, you may find that your physical health—intertwined with your mood—begins to improve. You may find that your mind is calmer and more even-keeled. Freshly liberated from psychological prison, the truth is working to set you free.

This is never a "free" ride though. You must keep working hard to exorcise the demons of past wounds and stay vigilant from falling into the old traps of darkness. Where Panel Three was an unsustainable, fixed, static, crippled, and atrophied *devolution*, Panel Eight is a self-generating, ever-growing, ever-flowing *evolution* of movement and change. Remember, health begets more health.

Knowing that our parents—and all of our multigenerational ancestors—were not the cause of Part One of their own lives, we can now see clearly that *their* light was blocked by the infiltrations passed down to *them* and forgive them for their unconscious parenting. Remember that this tragic multigenerational transference was not in vain if it served its curse-by-design purpose to end the transmission to you and the next generation.

Because you have worked so hard to elevate yourself to a higher state of consciousness, you are now compassionately able to mend the initial wounds of disconnect—between yourself and mother and/or father—and arrive at your final emancipation. Because you have healed your *now*, you are finally in the generous position of being able to heal the past and future generations—"backward and forward."

PANEL EIGHT: A VISUAL METAPHOR FOR YOUR HEALING

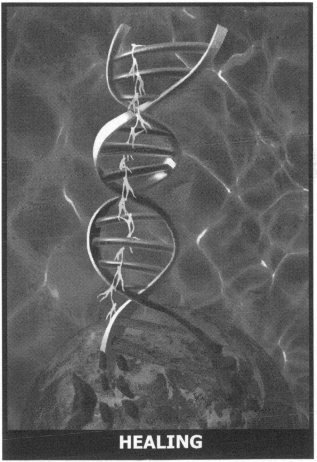

HEALING

Please study Panel Eight. Notice how the previously dismantled strands of Panel Four weave back into a single interconnected, reintegrated ribbon of DNA and have intertwined into a silvery white light of unity. This represents your healing *through* the process, *from* a fractured self, *to* wholeness. The DNA strand of the higher and lower rungs also symbolizes this backward and forward healing.

The restored, unsoiled DNA is also a metaphor for the healing of your pillars: one strand representing mother, the other, father. The intertwining of the two signifies the reintegration of the family unit as well

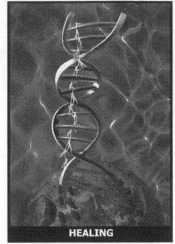

HEALING

as the rehabilitation of the core self. The new strand represents the new system and a release from the double dungeon of darkness.

The backdrop of water denotes both a PH balance—a neutrality of reactivity, or a washing away of the old—and an opportunity for a new beginning. Notice the details of beings helping each other up the rungs of psychospiritual evolution. Unlike the disconnected relationships in Panel Three, these beings embody different aspects of your evolving self and your expanding relationships.

Now better able to support yourself and your own needs, you are more capable of giving and receiving help from others. You can now reconnect as part of the team of humanity, integrating your past, present, and future. Panel Eight is a glimmering reminder that you are not alone and that you must conjoin with others in order to continue to grow and flourish. To maintain transformation, you have to share it. "I will invest in those who invest in me."

RELATIONSHIP GRIP

"Relationship grip" is our ability to hold onto and preserve healthy relationships and let go of those that don't serve us. Relationship grip allows us to use our new, healthy encoding to elevate ourselves and others as well as distinguish when to let go of people who pull us down.

Developing a healthier core self allows us to have the foundation to connect to and foster healthy relationships. Having a good "grip" on relationships is important in moving forward in life and making sure our future relationship choices help us evolve.

PONZI SCHEME RELATIONSHIPS

Charles Ponzi (March 3, 1882—January 18, 1949) was an Italian businessman and con artist in the U.S. and Canada. He promised clients a 50% profit within 45 days, or 100% profit within 90 days. In reality, Ponzi was paying early investors using the investments of later investors, a practice known as "robbing Peter to pay Paul." His scheme ran for over a year before it collapsed, costing his investors $20 million dollars.

Ponzi schemes—and other fraudulent, Ponzi-type relationships of betrayal—are common occurrences usually involving a sociopath and a codependent. The Ponzi schemer usually preys on a person that they know. The familiar and/or familial type of association is used to establish trust and lure the person in. This process is called "affinity fraud" because the victim feels an affinity toward the schemer. A Ponzi scheme relationship is an example of a relationship picker gone wrong. When we bond with people we think will help benefit us and end up feeling used at the end of the process, we must take the time to self-reflect on how we got hooked in the first place.

The "black widow," who, for example, preys on a wealthy man (or vice versa) is an example of a Ponzi-type relationship. The dynamics work like this: the "black widow" finds a vulnerable, usually much older man and entices him into marrying her by promising to care for him. As soon as she has a hook into his finances, she begins to flow a pipeline of his money into her own and her children's bank accounts, while assuming the role of a protective and loving wife.

The widower, who needs his emotional and oftentimes sexual desires fulfilled, throws his own children under the bus to keep the dysfunctional bond with her. When he dies, she inherits his money, and his family is left broke and betrayed.

The victims of such schemes are often people who are co-dependent, overly trusting, idealistic, and/or needy. When the perpetrator senses vulnerability, trust, and need, the "scheme" can be enacted.

Vulnerability can easily be established when the schemer preys on their victim's negative core belief. People who carry negative core beliefs—"I'm not special," or "I'm not good enough"—are particularly vulnerable to fall victim to the "special" deal that is only offered to "special" people.

THE WORD AS CAUSE

Words can connect. Words can disconnect. Our words are *causal*. The words and the language we use are the instruments that can trigger hurt, pain, chaos, and breakdown, or, on the contrary, can be used to mend.

Think of life enhancing words emanating from leaders such as Martin Luther King, who said, "The truth will set you free." Now, think of words from the mouth of a monster like Adolf Hitler, who said, "It is not truth that matters but victory." The first set of words inspires us to evolve, whereas the second set of words inspires destruction.

Think of critical, judgmental words from a parent to a child and their caustic effects versus words of kindness and support. Avram Noam Chomsky is an American linguist, philosopher, cognitive scientist, logician, political commentator, and social justice activist. Chomsky talked about the way we language. Chomsky said:

Language is a process of free creation; its laws and principles are fixed, but the manner in which the principles of generation are used is free and infinitely varied. Even the interpretation and use of words involves a process of free creation.

Our words act like a paintbrush, painting our reality. Sometimes they can act like scissors, cutting connection. Our words can sometimes be in the form of body language. Just like words, the messages can be connecting or disconnecting. For example, eye contact communicates that the person speaking is worth listening to, while being occupied with a cell phone and/or looking away can cause the speaker to feel like they don't matter. As you begin to be aware of the power of words and other forms of nonverbal communication, you can begin to decipher the connecting forms as well as the disconnecting ones.

KEEPING CONNECTED

To keep the connection and communicate the message, I created a communication tool I call the ***Peaceful Healing Dialogue*** (PHD). I originally created this dialogue so that couples could have a safe and effective way of communicating their feelings without disconnecting through judging, blaming, shaming, or criticizing each other. By learning the *Peaceful Healing Dialogue*, you can earn your Ph.D. in communication by expressing your thoughts and feelings *without* disconnecting emotionally.

The *Peaceful Healing Dialogue* is a powerful communication tool designed to prevent people from activating negative core beliefs and ripping open old wounds. The intention of the dialogue is to help express disagreements and/or hurt feelings through truthful, heartfelt conversations of compassion, empathy, and restoration.

PEACEFUL HEALING DIALOGUE (PHD)

"Relationships begin to weaken, then fail, when we stop doing the things that it took to get them in the first place."

- Always *R-E-S-P-E-C-T* each other.

- Always *BE TRUTHFUL*, even when it hurts.

- Always include *SELF-REFLECTION*—"Owning my own stuff."

- Always give the other person *HONEST, RIGOROUS FEEDBACK.*

- Offer *SOLUTIONS* on how to make things better.

- Keep each other *INTERCONNECTED*—not disconnected.

- Offer the other a chance to *ADDRESS THE ISSUES* that have caused the disconnect.

- *EXTEND A BRIDGE* back to one another.

- Be *ETHICAL, TRANSPARENT,* and *VULNERABLE.*

- Give each other a way to *SAY, "NO"* to any part of the relationship.

- *RENEGOTIATE* or *RESHUFFLE* the old system and *"UPDATE THE FILES".*

- Be *KIND* and *COMPASSIONATE* even when both partners do not agree. *No blaming, shaming, criticizing, or judging.*

- *GENTLY SHARE* with one another how the relationship is not working.

- Both partners must want to work on *INTERCONNECTION—RECONNECTION—UNITY*

Sometimes the dialogue leads to **P**eaceful **H**ealing **D**elight or sometimes to **P**eaceful **H**ealing **D**eparture/**D**ivorce

Cindy and Roberta Continued.

As you watched the transformation between Cindy's relationship with her mother Roberta, you witnessed a paradigm shift in Cindy's core belief and a relation-*shift* between mother and daughter. It is only over time that we can truly say that people *shifted.*

Upon her two year follow-up, Cindy reported that she was back in school and passionately pursuing her career as a hair stylist. She shared that her relationship with her daughter Kate is very connected, as is her relationship with her husband. In the course of the two years, she said that she dropped 20 pounds and no longer experiences symptoms of depression.

Roberta and Cindy have healthier boundaries and use the *Peaceful Healing Dialogue* to communicate, stay connected, and mend the occasional disconnects. Their dynamics have shifted, and as a result, Cindy is independent and has a strong voice of her own.

Roberta, no longer having to live her life through her daughter, has developed her own career, hobbies, and other interests. She is exercising more, eating right, and enjoying her newfound independence from the enmeshed relationship they once had.

White Roses Mother's Day was a symbol of healing and renewal. No longer are Cindy and Roberta connected by pathology. They have both worked to sever the dysfunctional mother-daughter bond and are actively re-coding and reshaping their relationship.

Whether or not your mother and/or father are still living or are estranged from you, having the opportunity to speak these words out loud and direct them at some version of your parents—actual or imaginary—is extremely powerful and liberating. This process allows you to come full circle and *truly* forgive, accept, and honor thy father and mother.

Mom and/or Dad, because of you:

I accept myself, put myself first, have clear boundaries, have peace, can stand up for myself, no longer feel like a victim.

Now is the time when we look back over the entire expedition and see just how far over the rainbow you and I have traveled together.

When you became disconnected from your mother and/or father, the world became a world of duality—black and white. Unable to conceptualize bad or good, impressions were still made on you and your psyche at a preverbal age.

Just as all children do, you longed for connection, dreaming of going "over the rainbow" to a place of hope and renewal, where "birds fly free" and where clouds of doubt and confusion are "far behind me," a time when you still had hope for a happier outcome for your life and *dared* to dream. As you discovered, it takes courage, support, the right environment and even a little bit of audacity to pursue and fulfill your dreams.

TRACKING THE JOURNEY THUS FAR

Dorothy's journey—a metaphor for your own journey—can be seen as a wisdom journey *from-through-to*. We discovered that the promise of an all-powerful Wizard is a symbol of our parents and the false gods we look to for salvation: money, fame, knowledge, sex, power, and even our parents. When we strip away the mask, the Wizard and our parents are just mortals pretending to be more, holding no true rewards that weren't already hidden within us all along. And in this way, all of us get to see— just as you have experienced—that our own liberation already lies within ourselves, given we are willing to clear out our past to make room for the future.

Three taps of her ruby slippers and Dorothy and Toto are back in Kansas. Dorothy is changed. Transformed. Knowing and wiser. And surrounded by those she loves. Whether it was a dream or her perception of reality, her consciousness shifted; the old paradigm is dead.

We each must travel down our own yellow-brick-road to enlightenment. But we do not have to do this completely alone. A new paradigm—a deliberate and essential shift and purification into a higher consciousness—is our only pathway to survival, both individually and collectively as a human race.

THINK LIKE A SHRINK: CONNECTING THE DOTS

- Letting go of the old coding allows you to Be The Cause® of new encoding.
- You can "recode" yourself with a more accurate, life-affirming, and positive core belief.
- As you heal, you may find that your physical health, intertwined with your mood, begins to improve.
- Having a good "grip" on relationships is important in moving forward in life.
- Remember, as health begets more health, you can…

Be The Cause® of better outcomes for your life!

PANEL NINE

TO THE SOLUTION: RECODING

UNITY

"Imagine there's no countries; It isn't hard to do. Nothing to kill or die for, and no religion too...
Imagine all the people living life in peace."
~ John Lennon

From your dark and wounded past, *through* the process of dismantling your negative core beliefs, you have come full circle *to* healing your internal world. Now more balanced and sustainable, you have more to share, not only with others in your immediate circle but with the world around you as well. As we heal individually, we can heal globally.

Please study Panel Nine. Think of Planet Earth as a metaphor for Mother Earth, mother, or source of life. Notice that Planet Earth is immersed in water, a metaphor for purifying, neutralizing and cleansing—a washing away of the darkness of the multigenerational wounds and their collective effects on the entire planet. Think of Panel Nine as your blank slate for re-creation—your clean start.

As you recall from Panel One, the health of your mother is interconnected with your well-being. When your mother is healthy and feeds you the nutrients you need to develop emotionally and physically, you have more opportunity to flourish. As you attain more health in mind, body, and soul and no longer feel trapped in your double dungeon of darkness, you may find that your relationship with Mother Earth improves.

169

PANEL NINE: A VISUAL METAPHOR
FOR YOUR UNITY

UNITY

Look intently at the dolphins in Panel Nine and notice the three dolphins at the bottom of the Panel. They represent your wisdom messengers reminding you that your fractured vision of yourself and others is just an illusion—that your state of consciousness is the *cause* of the outcome of your life—and that we are all interconnected.

Our mental health is a reflection of how we treat Mother Earth. Our suffering and fractured humanity reflect our collective state of mental un-health and the extent to which we are poisoned—mind, body, and soul.

When we are not well, we project our pain onto Mother Earth and then proverbially "drink" from her polluted waters.

As we become healthier collectively, we become more eco-friendly, no longer needing to project our un-health onto our environment. As we heal, Mother Earth can heal and replenish as well. The beauty of nature can then begin to reflect back our state of health.

FROM COLLECTIVE UNCONSCIOUS *TO* COLLECTIVE CONSCIOUS

Swiss psychologist Carl Jung talked about the collective unconscious and how we are intricately interconnected:

It must be pointed out that just as the human body shows a common anatomy over and above all racial differences, so, too, the psyche possesses a common substratum transcending all differences in culture and consciousness. I have called this substratum the collective unconscious.

When you look at the world at large, you can see that we have created a global double dungeon. With the constant threat of nuclear war and daily threats of violence, we have collectively gone beyond the metaphor of darkness of our personal double dungeon, manifesting it into our world. Whether we like it or not, we are interconnected. We share the same air, soil, and water. Spiritually we share the same soul. If we are one, then how we treat others is how we treat our collective selves.

As *causal* beings we can choose to turn our collective unconscious into a collective "conscious" and choose to act synergistically. As we open up the chambers of our collective double dungeon we can re-*cause*, or re-project, a new form of consciousness into the world based on peace, wisdom, health, and unity. The choice is ours.

Healing Human Disconnect is the first step towards Healing Global Disconnect. The warring factions of nation against nation— manifestations of our collective injuries—represent on a macro scale our hatred and intolerance of ourselves, our families, significant others, and the world at large.

"The greatness of a nation can be judged by the way its animals are treated."
~Mahatma Gandhi

Chloe
Internal Racism

"Chloe," in her early 30's, is half African-American and half Caucasian. She came to see me because she hated the blackness within herself. This self-racism is not uncommon yet not spoken about enough. Chloe represents the double dungeon of her darkness from within, reinforced by a world that is still a hostile and unwelcoming environment for people who don't fit the mold.

Chloe, who was interested in pursuing law, went into great detail researching studies about how black women are viewed by non-blacks of the opposite sex. She was on a mission to prove her point and core belief that she is "ugly and unlovable".

Her findings confirmed that the vast majority of black women are the least desirable choice for the majority of men. Because she placed all value of how men see her on her statistics, she felt disheartened about finding a relationship.

"I've been working on this case (of self-hatred) for a long time," she said in therapy. Trapped in her double dungeon of low self-esteem and in a society that, according to her research, found black women sexually least desirable, she felt that she had no place to turn. Chloe wished to "cut" the black features "out" of her physical self. If not for the fear of the knife, she would have preferred to be at a plastic surgeon's office rather than in my office. She admitted that she wanted to die and would have committed suicide if not for her fear of the methods it would take to end her life and the trauma it would cause her siblings and family.

Chloe's parents separated when she was three years old. When her white mother and black father split up, the union of the "white queen" and the "black king"—our chess metaphor—resulted in a split of her kingdom. While united, she felt safe in her mixed ethnicity. When her parents split up, it was as though the safety net broke, and she fell into the unwelcoming hands of the white society.

I decided to cross-examine her primary negative core belief, and she agreed not to use false evidence against herself. She promised to be fair. She went as far as to say that "all people who are black or half black are ugly, and if they feel good about themselves, they should get out of denial as soon as possible and face the grim reality of the statistics. They need a course to correct their 'distorted' self -perception."

I asked Chloe if she was willing to conduct this course. She turned to me and said, "This is a course in suicide!" I asked her if she herself was enrolled in this course, and she said yes. She clearly needed to be checkmated out of her pathology.

Chloe was in a *triple dungeon of darkness*. She hated herself, and according to her statistics, the world hated her too. Her statistical proof created the final set of bars that locked her into the dungeon and threw away her key to freedom. Over her lifetime, more bars and more layers came down.

She was an enemy unto herself. Chloe's inner world is a sad example of our outer world fractured into *isms*—races, nations, religions, politics, philosophies. The world is clearly not prepared for our mixed-race world, and we are having a tough time blending. We need more systems to help us as a human race transition from a divided humanity to a blended one.

Chloe's injury from a *causal* viewpoint is that her parents not only did not stay united as a couple but also did not prepare her for this racially divided world. She did not ask to be born, and now she felt forced to cope with forces beyond her control. She wished her parents had prepared her for the harsh realities of the world concerning her race. In 5th grade, she recalled the boy she had a crush on asking her why her skin was "poop colored." When she came home in tears, her mom simply dismissed the interaction as a "silly boy who was just talking nonsense." No further guidance was provided. Others constantly asked about her curly hair and made comments about her lips. Her last relationship ended when her boyfriend's family members referred to him as a "nigger-lover" for dating her. Although she was, as she said, "light-skinned," she still faced these problems "because being black isn't about *just* the color of your skin. It's all about the features. I can't hide beyond my skin tone." She was constantly facing negative reaffirmations of how undesirable it is to be black.

Sealed and done. The infiltrations had won. Her goal today is to get out of her own triple dungeon by becoming a light for the world.

FRACTURED HUMANITY OR UNITY:
THE CHOICE IS OURS

As we come full circle and revisit Ralph Waldo Emerson's quote about our global state of affairs and *"the reason why the world lacks unity and lies broken and in heaps,"* we can now have a deeper understanding that the reason man became *"disunited with himself"* has to do with Human Disconnect, beginning with mother-infant disconnect. Now "gone viral," our fractured state of global disconnect can be understood as a magnification of our collective individual wounds.

The better we heal individually, the better we *can*—and *must*—heal globally; otherwise, we *will* perish. The choice is ours, and our challenge is to apply our newfound wisdom to create a paradigm of thinking that fosters an inclusionary way of co-existing in peace.

As we clear out our infiltrated past, we can extend our well-being to the entire human race and begin to heal globally. Only after we heal individually can we more intentionally and more powerfully begin to focus on global healing.

HOW TO KEEP OUR WORLD INFILTRATION FREE

Just like preventing cancer cells from taking over the body by staying healthy, we can be proactive and self-correct before we fall into a "death code" consciousness of criticism, shame, blame, and judgment. By staying vigilant about our state of consciousness, we can stop its manifestation into our collective consciousness, averting our global demise.

It is no coincidence that the word *compassion* contains the word *passion*. Compassion is a state of grace, a state of being able to put oneself into another's shoes. Compassion does not mean sweeping injurious behaviors under the rug. It requires holding the other person accountable to the process of self-reflecting and self-correcting. Through compassion and empathy, you can attenuate the projection process and help others to take responsibility for their thoughts and behaviors.

When projections stop, feeling judged stops, allowing for faster self-reflection and self-correction. By creating more compassionate systems of relating to one another, we can regain our passion and purpose and be back in the flow.

JOIN THE HUMAN RACE

What is possible for us as a human race when we stop reacting to our original wounds? What is possible for us when we no longer project our pain onto others and our planet? What is possible once we can feel compassion for our primary caregivers and *their* caregivers?

Thank you for joining me on this journey of healing. You have journeyed *from* the problem, *through* the process, *to* the solution, and are now aware that healing is a lifelong process.

It is my hope that, after reading this book, you have a better understanding of the importance of self-expression as a gateway to mental health, a better and deeper understanding of the destructive nature of criticism, shame, blame, and judgment, and a better understanding of the importance of self-reflection and self–correction as a way to evolve. It is my hope that you are more conscious and aware of how your curse-by-design challenges were elegantly tailored to help you to morph and grow. It is my hope that you join the human race through becoming more inclusionary and humane.

FORGIVENESS AND COMPASSION

Now that you have done much of the work of releasing the poisons from the wounds of the past, I invite you to begin the final phase of your journey: the phase of compassionate forgiveness for your mother and father and all your caregivers from your present and past generations.

As your inner world begins to harmonize, you may find that you can begin to feel a sense of compassion for yourself, your caregivers, and all injured souls who live in their own personal double dungeon of darkness. Forgiveness is a lifetime process and there will be times when forgiveness seems illusive and impossible. Remember to forgive yourself for being imperfect in your inability to forgive perfectly.

Please remember that you are part of a web of interconnectivity and that through the power of unconditional love—the most powerful healing force on the planet—you can continue to Be The Cause of manifesting better outcomes for your life, for the lives of those around you, and for the lives of future generations.

Thank you for allowing me to guide you through this journey to heal Human Disconnect. In conclusion, I would like to invite you to remember and pay forward to future generations my vision and dream for a united humanity. With that, I would like to leave you with visionary/songwriter John Lennon's message …

Imagine all the people
Sharing all the world...
You may say I'm a dreamer
But I'm not the only one.
I hope someday you'll join us
And the world will live as one.

THINK LIKE A SHRINK: CONNECTING THE DOTS

- As you heal individually, we can heal globally.
- We have to hold each other accountable for stopping negative consciousness before it manifests itself into our collective demise.
- Our mental health is a reflection of how we treat Mother Earth and our animals.
- Compassion does not mean sweeping injurious behavior under the rug.
- Healing and forgiveness is a lifelong process.
- Your "curse-by-design" was elegantly tailored to challenge you to morph and grow so that you can...

Be The Cause® of better outcomes for your life!

GLOSSARY

DR. JUDY-ISMS AND OTHER KEY TERMS

Acts of Commission: Abuse committed by the abuser.

Acts of Omission: Abuse by virtue of standing by and doing nothing to stop the abuse.

Anti-Mommies/Daddies: Psychological protection from wounds our parents inflict on us.

Attachment Theory: Dr. John Bowlby's theory on how mental health is formed. Through secure mother-infant, father-infant, and family attachment and connection, the blueprint for mental health is created. The basic ingredients for mental health include breast-feeding, attuning to the child, consistent parenting, and prioritizing the needs of the child.

Be The Cause®: The purpose of the Mind Map™ System—to shift you out of being at the *effect* of your life to being the *cause* of your life. When you become the *cause*, you proactively and intentionally shift your consciousness to Be The Cause of better outcomes for your life.

Big *I*: Your light. Your full potential and highest form of self. You have the potential to self-actualize into your Big *I* when given psychological and physical ingredients required for growth.

Cause: Your original blueprint , your family of origin, and your multigenerational family. When referring to the *cause*, I am referring to the people who blueprinted you, typically your primary and secondary caregivers—mother and father.

Childhood Is A Hostage Situation: As children, we don't choose our parents and we are hostages to our parent's parenting skills or lack thereof. We are at the *effect* of their treatment of us.

Complex PTSD: Otherwise known as Complex Post Traumatic Stress Disorder, or Disorders of Extreme Stress Not Otherwise Specified. An outcome of long-term effects of childhood physical abuse, sexual abuse, or exposure to domestic violence, triggering exaggerated responses to reminders of the original trauma.

Consciousness: Intention—where you're coming *from*, so to speak. Consciousness is *causal*. Your consciousness determines whether you will end up in Panels Four-Five-Six (Chaos, Defenses, and Breakdowns) or Panels Seven-Eight-Nine (Paradigm Shift, Healing, and Unity).

Cracked Lens of Perception: Childhood wounds crack our psychoperceptual lens, warping our ability to see ourselves and the world around us with clear perception. As a result, we feel like we are "cracking up."

Critical Mass: The tipping point between destruction and rebirth.

Curse-By-Design: Wounds of childhood that become our challenges and opportunities for psychospiritual growth.

Darkness: Our unconscious shadows from wounds of childhood. Human Disconnect creates darkness. When we are disconnected *from*, we emotionally short circuit and experience darkness.

***Dis*-ease**: We are born whole and complete. When we are injured and disconnected *from*, we are no longer at ease—we are at *dis*-ease.

Double Dungeon of Darkness: When we are not given psychological nourishment from either mother or father and can't turn to either parent because they are not emotionally or physically available, we experience feelings of emptiness, darkness, loneliness, and a sense of hopelessness. We feel locked in the double dungeon of darkness.

Effect: When we are unconscious, we are at the *effect* of. When we have no power or control over our lives, we are at the *effect* of. Childhood as hostage situation is an example.

Enlightened Witness: A clear seeing person who stands witness to your childhood trauma and helps you understand that you are not crazy but have been made to think you are crazy by the insanity of the situation.

Flying Monkeys: A term borrowed from *The Wizard of Oz*. Individuals who do other people's evil bidding.

Gaslighting: A term borrowed from a film titled *Gas Light*—a form of manipulation that seeks to sow seeds of doubt about our perception and sanity.

Global Disconnect: Oppressive, discriminatory ideologies that fracture our interconnectedness and create macro disconnection within the human race.

Healing Backward: Healing past multigenerational wounds.

Healing Forward: Preventing wounds of childhood from embedding and infecting future generations.

Hostage Situation: A situation where there is no control or escape. Childhood is an example of a hostage situation.

Human Disconnect: The cause of most inorganic psychopathology. Human Disconnect starts with mother-infant disconnect and creates pain and suffering.

Isms: Oppressive, discriminatory ideologies that fracture our interconnectedness. Isms also refer to our defense mechanisms, mechanisms used to help shield us from the pain of Human Disconnect.

Labelism: Using labels to describe a problem when in truth the label is the outcome of the problem.

Light: Consciousness, being conscious, health, wholeness. When we connect with ourselves, our families our communities, and with the world at large, we reconnect with our light. From a psychospiritual perspective, when we connect to Source, we connect to light.

Little *I*: The injured self. The reduced self. When we are wounded, we cannot manifest the best of our best. Childhood injuries make it is more difficult to self-actualize and grow into the person we were intended to be.

Mind Map: The Be The Cause Mind Map is a pathway *from* identifying old childhood wounds, *through* dismantling their effects on your psyche, *to* paradigm shifting you into health.

Multigenerational Transmission Process: Family generations of psychological un-health passed from one generation to the next. Unhealed parental wounds transmit to the next generation.

Nature: Our genetics make-up is our nature. For example, our genetics determine our eye color, height, etc. Our genetics are more hardwired, although they interact with nurture to determine the outcome.

Negative Core Beliefs: Core beliefs we encode into our belief system about ourselves and the world based on how we were treated as children. They are based on lies and misinformation.

Nurture: Through nurture we either evolve or devolve. Nurture is *causal*. When we are not nurtured properly it affects us on all levels—emotionally, physically and spiritually. Nurture and nature interact to determine the outcome of our lives.

Part One of Our Lives: Before we were conscious of being at the *effect* of childhood wounds. Before healing and becoming *causal*.

Part Two of Our Lives: After we become conscious of the multigenerational "system gone wrong," after healing our childhood wounds we can Be The Cause® of creating better outcomes for our life.

Peaceful Healing Dialogue (PHD): A way of communicating to keep the connection and get the message across. The Peaceful Healing Dialogue is intended to help heal human disconnect.

Precipice: Being at the edge, or at the pivotal point of a major life choice.

Psycho-Viruses: Messages from your family of origin penetrate into your psyche, or the fiber of your being. These viruses infect your thinking, propagate, and take over your mental health. If not destroyed and dismantled, they will pass on to the next generation.

Self-Reflect/Self-Correct: The process of looking inward and taking responsibility for your part in the disconnections you create, then self-correcting in order to heal the disconnect. The Peaceful Healing Dialogue is a way of communicating to repair human disconnect through self-reflecting and self-correcting.

Source: God, creation, the *light*, universal energy, universal truth.

System Gone Wrong: A psychological system that has been derailed because of multigenerational injuries.

Think Like A Shrink: Your goal is to learn how to analyze the source of your pain, recognize your patterns, and sustain your mental health for life.

Truth Conversations: A series of therapeutic conversations designed to process your wounds of childhood, get the psychological poison of the past out of your system, and heal.

WTF (What The Freud!): Over-the-top, repetitive, unconscious, and exaggerated reactions to triggers of unhealed childhood wounds. When these wounds are reopened, they domino into Chaos, Defenses, and Breakdowns—Panels Four, Five, and Six. WTF reactions make the person appear crazy in the context of the situation.

Wound Activation Prevention System: A system designed to help you process your raw amygdala, reactionary feelings so that you can regain your emotional equilibrium.

REFERENCES AND NOTES

Adler, W. (2004). *The War of the Roses*. Sourcebooks, Inc.

Bowen, M. (1993). *Family Therapy in Clinical Practice*. Jason Aronson.

Bowlby, J. (1978). Attachment theory and its therapeutic implications. *Adolescent Psychiatry, 6*, 5-33.

Capra, F. (1983). *The Turning Point: Science, Society, and the Rising Culture*. Bantam.

Childre, D. L., Martin, H., & Beech, D. (1999). *The HeartMath Solution: The Institute of HeartMath's Revolutionary Program for Engaging the Power of the Heart's Intelligence*. HarperOne.

Csikszentmihalyi, Mihaly. *Flow: The Psychology of Optimal Experience*. New York: Harper & Row, 1990.

Duarte, E. (2012). Plato's "Allegory of the Cave". In *Being and Learning* (pp. 69-106). SensePublishers.

Einstein, Albert. "*What Life Means to Einstein: An Interview by George Sylvester Viereck*" The Saturday Evening Post (26 October 1929).

Ellis, A. (2001). *Overcoming Destructive Beliefs, Feelings, and Behaviors: New Directions for Rational Emotive Behavior Therapy*. Prometheus Books.

Freud, S., & Strachey, J. (1991). *Beyond the Pleasure Principle* (Vol. 18). Hogarth Press.

Gordon, A. K. (2003). *Tibetan Religious Art*. Courier Corporation.

Hamilton, Patrick (1938). *Gas Light. A Screenplay*

Hebb, D. O. (1949). *The Organization of Behavior: A Neuropsychological Approach*. John Wiley & Sons.

Jung, C. G. (1958). *Psyche and Symbol: A Selection from the Writings of CG Jung* (Vol. 136). Anchor Books.

Kübler-Ross, E., Wessler, S., & Avioli, L. V. (1972). On Death and Dying. *Jama 221*(2), 174-179.

Larson, B. M. (2005). The war of the roses: demilitarizing invasion biology. *Frontiers in Ecology and the Environment, 3*(9), 495-500.

Mahler, M. S. (1968). *On Human Symbiosis and the Vicissitudes of Individuation. Infantile Psychosis, Volume 1.*

Maslow, A. H. (1950). Self-actualizing people: a study of psychological health. *Personality.*

Masterson, J. F., & Klein, R. (Eds.). (2013). *Disorders of the Self: New Therapeutic Horizons: the Masterson Approach*. Routledge.

Matt, D. C. (1983). *Zohar, the Book of Enlightenment*. Paulist Press.

Miller, A. (1997). *The Drama of the Gifted Child: The Search for the True Self.* Basic Books.

Mones, P. (1991). *When a Child Kills*. New York: Pocket Books.

Planck, Max. J. W. N. Sullivan, *Observer*, 25 January 1931, p. 17.

Plato. (1945). *The Republic of Plato* (Vol. 30, pp. 175-203). New York: Oxford University Press.

Rosenberg, J. (2014). *Lucid Darkness*. Psychological Healing Center.

Schore, A. N. (2002). Dysregulation of the right brain: a fundamental mechanism of traumatic attachment and the psychopathogenesis of posttraumatic stress disorder. *Australian and New Zealand Journal of Psychiatry, 36*(1), 9-30.

Singer, T. (2006). The neuronal basis and ontogeny of empathy and mind reading: review of literature and implications for future research. *Neuroscience & Biobehavioral Reviews, 30*(6), 855-863.

Tatkin, S. (2012). *Wired for Love: How Understanding Your Partner's Brain and Attachment Style Can Help You Defuse Conflict and Build a Secure Relationship.* New Harbinger Publications.

Thurman, R. (2011). *Tibetan Book of the Dead.* Bantam.

Tolle, E., & Tolle, E. (2001). *Practicing the Power of Now: Essential Teachings, Meditations, and Exercises from the Power of Now.* Novato, CA: New World Library.

Winnicott, D. W. (1953). (1953). Transitional Objects and Transitional Phenomena—A Study of the First Not-Me Possession. *International Journal of Psycho-Analysis, 34,* 89-97.

ABOUT THE AUTHOR

Dr. Judy Rosenberg is a licensed clinical psychologist, founder of the **Psychological Healing Center®** and creator of the **Be The Cause® Mind Map™ System for Healing Human Disconnect®**. By helping people identify the *cause* of emotional pain and suffering and dismantle it at its inception, Dr. Judy and her team of therapists help people paradigm shift into better mental health.

Dr. Rosenberg has been interviewed by several television shows including MTV, CBS, KCAL News, National Enquirer TV, Blind Date, Animal Planet, Huffington Post, and E! Entertainment. She has been featured in several prominent newspapers such as the Wall Street Journal, the Hollywood Reporter, Men's Health, and People Magazine. She has been in private practice as a clinical psychologist since 1996.

Dr. Judy hosts a radio show on UBN Radio every Thursday at 8pm PST titled **Dr. Judy WTF—What The Freud!** Topics center around healing the *hole in the soul* that Human Disconnect leaves us with. The show focuses on going global, deeper, and cross-cultural.

Dr. Judy is currently in private practice in Sherman Oaks and Beverly Hills, California. She and her team help people with a multitude of psychological issues heal cross-culturally and globally both in person and via Teletherapy. She also trains other professionals in her Mind Map™ System.

HEALING GLOBALLY

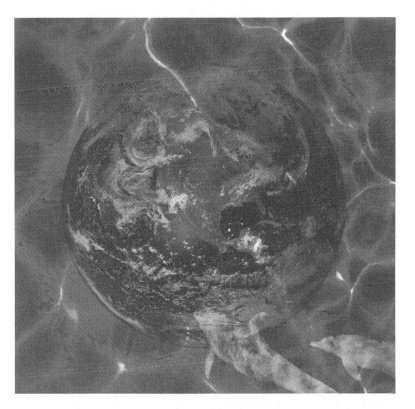

As a human race, we have become fragmented into nations, religions, social classes, politics, and races. This fragmentation has resulted in clash and fallout in the form of human atrocities.

Although we have been able to soar to unlimited heights in many areas of human endeavor, we have yet to accomplish the final and most important frontier: to come together as a united humanity.

Once we heal individually, we can begin to heal globally. To join Dr. Judy in this mission, visit ***HealingGlobalDisconnect.com***.®

OTHER BOOKS BY DR. JUDY

Lucid Darkness

The peaceful life of Los Angeles psychologist Dr. Livia Abrams is about to take a dangerous and deadly turn. Armed with only a conceptual roadmap for Healing Human Disconnect and her own bold resolve, Livia is suddenly thrust into the volatile world of the Gaza Strip as her ambitious theories on shifting global consciousness aren't the only things about to catch fire.

LUCID DARKNESS is an unflinching, relentless psychological thriller that will have you at the edge of the cliff and at the edge of your seat. Get ready for a daring, suspenseful, and explosive journey into the darkness.

Available at Amazon.com

Dr. Judy's Habit Breakers, Stop Smoking Plan

In Dr. Judy's Habit Breakers Stop Smoking Plan, she provides a plan and the tools to help you quit smoking and stay smoke-free. The Plan details two key tools integral to your success: The Be The Cause Mind Map, a paradigm shifting system that will take you *from* your addiction, *through* your de-addiction, and *to* freedom and healing; and an e-Cigarette plan to successfully transition you from smoker to ex-smoker. Dr. Judy's Habit Breakers Stop Smoking Plan confronts all the problems that confront you: the chemical and psychological addiction to nicotine, the nagging urge to smoke, ways to relax without smoking, weight gain, relapse triggers, the need for ongoing support. Dr. Judy helps you say goodbye to smoking as you build your desire for health and lose the desire to resume your unhealthy and destructive habit.

Available at Amazon.com

BE THE CAUSE: NINE PANEL MIND MAP VIDEO JOURNEY TO HEALING

Dr. Judy's Mind Map™ Video Series Will Teach You to *Think Like A Shrink* and Be The Cause® of Creating Better Outcomes for Your Life!

Get To The Truth:
Identify Your Childhood Wounds
Learn how to identify childhood wounds from your past, how you reacted to them, and how you encoded them into your being.

See How Your Wounds Still Affect You Today: See how your wounds created your current chaos and how to identify defense mechanisms that keep you stuck. Break *through* your defenses and release yourself from psychological prison.

Learn To Shift: *Paradigm Shift Into Mental Health*
Learn how to paradigm shift your relationship with yourself and others, heal, recode, and reconnect. This will allow you to Be The Cause® of better outcomes for your life.

Save time, money, and do your Mind Map™ process in the privacy of your own home on your own schedule. Heal through a proven System that thousands of clients have participated in and have successfully used to paradigm shift into mental health.

The Mind Map™ System is designed to *HEAL HUMAN DISCONNECT®* and dismantle your *dis*-ease, or symptoms, and damaging patterns of mental un-health at the *CAUSAL* level. Unlike traditional therapy, it is time limited to 10 sessions and effectively identifies your *WOUNDS OF CHILDHOOD*, how they *EMBED* into your psyche, and how to HEAL by shifting out of your old, unhealthy psychological blueprint, rebooting the system, and creating a new, sustainable, healthy future.

Available at ***PsychologicalHealingCenter.com/video-series***

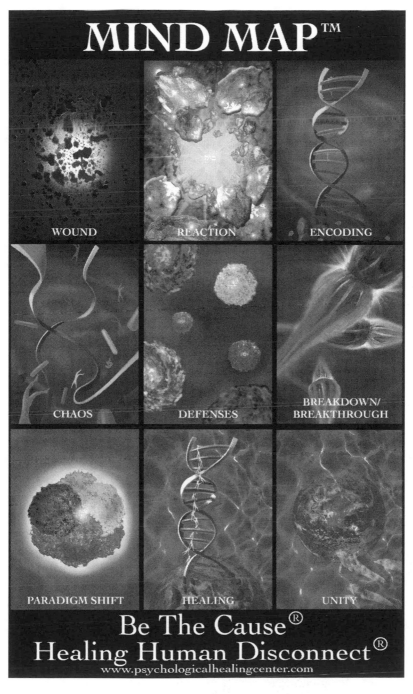

For full color Mind Map, please visit
PsychologicalHealingCenter.com/get-mind-map

Made in the USA
Las Vegas, NV
06 January 2024

83984772R00107